Crybabies

Crybabies

Coping with Colic:
What to Do
When Baby
Won't Stop
Crying

by
MARC WEISSBLUTH, M.D.

This book is dedicated to
Linda, Daniel, Michael, Jed, *and* **Elliott,**
who taught me how to love children.

Published in the United Stated of America by Arbor House Publishing Company and in Canada by Fitzhenry & Whiteside, Ltd.

Library of Congress Cataloging in Publication Data

Weissbluth, Marc.
  Crybabies.

  Bibliography: p.
  1. Colic.   2. Crying.   3. Infants — Care and hygiene.
I.Title.
RJ456.C7W45   1984   618.92'33   84-2826
ISBN 0-87795-611-1

Manufactured in the United States of America

10 9 8 7 6 5 4 3 2 1

This book is printed on acid free paper. The paper in this book meets the guidelines for permanence and durability of the Committee on Production Guidelines for Book Longevity of the Council on Library Resources.

Contents

Introduction

You can't send your crybaby back.

But admit it, there are times when you wish you could. If your baby is among the one-fifth who has colic, he or she is putting you through a trying and confusing time. You may face hours of screaming every day. You may feel that your baby is beyond your reach. You may not be getting much rest. You may feel guilty, angry, or just unlucky. You may not really understand what is happening, or why. This book is for you.

It is also for health-care professionals who deal with colicky babies and their parents. I have tried to achieve a balance between technical and nontechnical information, so that people both with and without medical training can benefit from it. I will be presenting research studies done on colic and related problems. I trust that professionals will not think that I have oversimplified the conclusions, just as I hope parents will not be overburdened with the data. Colic has to be approached on both the practical and the theoretical fronts, and that is what this book does.

7

My First Experience with Colic

I was a medical student when my first son was born. He cried and cried for hours on end. Neither my wife nor I thought this was strange. We assumed that all babies behaved this way. No one told us, fortunately, that he had a "condition." We didn't know enough to worry that it might be because he was a boy, or our firstborn, or breastfed, or that we were unwittingly making him miserable. Maybe the complete absence of teaching about colic in medical school was a blessing for us.

I remember rocking my son for hours on end while trying to memorize neuroanatomy. I would sometimes pretend to close my eyes, hoping he would do the same, but every time I peeked, he had his radar-beam gaze fixed on me. Calming him down always took an hour or two of rocking. Once he began breathing deeply and regularly in my arms I could put him down in his crib. But if I was impatient and tried to put him down before this deep sleep developed, he would arch his back, open his eyes wide, and start to cry once again.

My wife was studying Dostoevsky or Old Church Slavonic, which is harder than neuroanatomy. We took turns pacing, walking, rocking. In our student apartment, my son's room was above the postage stamp-sized kitchen. I remember unwashed dinner dishes piled up late into the night because the slightest banging would awaken our little angel. Looking back, I think we were too tired and preoccupied with our studies to worry much about his behavior. But I have never felt the same about neuroanatomy.

If this routine sounds familiar to you, you might like to know that things settled down for us within a few months. Our son became a delightful baby. Our three subsequent children had no excessive crying. I most likely would not even remember those first noisy months had I not developed a special interest, as a pediatrician and researcher, in colic.

Colic is what that was, although I didn't call it that at the time. There is some question about whether giving a label to a pattern of behavior like this makes it seem better or worse. Some parents are relieved to know that this kind of crying is so common that it's called something. Others feel that, as one mother told me, "Once you give it a name, it's a *real* problem." A father was perfectly willing to admit that his young daughter cried and screamed for hours on end, but emphatically denied that she could have colic. If parents would rather think they just have a very fussy baby, this is fine. For, as we shall see, the line between normal crying behavior and "colic" is an arbitrary one. When does sadness become depression? When does overweight become obesity? When does intelligence become genius? Crying becomes colic when the researchers doing the defining say it does.

All babies cry some of the time and most parents are not sure how to handle it. This book will tell you what to do when your baby cries. The first step is to understand what we know about infant crying and colic.

Chapter 1

What Is Colic?

Colic is a puzzle, and I do not claim to have solved it. This is not the sort of book which has a story to sell. You will find no sweeping theories, startling discoveries, or three-step solutions. You will find a summary of everything that is known or believed about colic right now. I believe that the more you know about colic, the less worried you will be.

I will begin with definitions of colic. You will want to know right off if this could be your child's problem. Most child-care books and many doctors, too, are quite vague about colic, so you may have found it hard to decide.

Because colic is different things to different people, and because factual information has been scarce and inconclusive, many "explanations" have evolved through the years. Some of them are repeated as fact, even by doctors and nurses. Totally ineffectual treatments are often recommended. One of my purposes here is to separate myth from fact. I will be examining the most common old wives' tales about colic, the ones your parents have probably already heard from helpful relatives and friends. Then I will review what we actually know about colic, based on properly conducted experiments reported in professional journals.

I will offer suggestions on coping with colic which have helped hundreds of my patients. Procedures range from rocking to drugs to getting out of the house for an evening. I will talk about preventing colic from turning into a long-term behavioral sleeping problem, and how to solve that problem if it occurs.

I will also offer some intriguing new theories on colic. In the past few years, a number of studies have pointed to links connecting colicky behavior; a certain kind of infant temperament, sleep habits, and such body functions as control of breathing during sleep. I have brought together here for the first time a number of these studies which I think shed light on the colic mystery, even though in many cases the original researchers did not have the idea of colic anywhere in their minds as they did their work. It does not make a tidy package yet—there is much work to do—but I feel the answer to the colic mystery lies in this direction.

I am also publishing here, for the first time outside of medical journals, the surprising results of a recent study of colicky infants done by some colleagues and me in 1982. Our results are exciting because they offer strong evidence that colic and its frequent aftermaths—fussy temperament and sleep disturbances—may all be part of one physiologically caused syndrome and not be due, as had been theorized, to the behavior of the child's parents.

Defining the Condition

Some doctors maintain that colic, by definition, must involve spells of violent, rhythmical screaming. Other doctors say it is not colic unless the baby's legs are drawn up and he seems to expel gas. Some doctors use the timing of the condition—the way the spells usually start about two weeks of age, end around three months, and are worst in the evening—as the indication of colic. A few researchers claim that only babies who are ill-tempered and fussy all their waking hours can be called colicky. On the other hand, one of the earliest students of colic wrote, "The outstanding impression given by the colicky baby, except in the evening, is that he is a well, thriving, well-fed and well-managed baby with nothing wrong with him."

So let us use a broad definition. This book, when it uses the term "colic," means: inconsolable crying for which no physical cause can be found, which lasts more than three hours a day, occurs at least three days a week and continues for at least three weeks.

Let's examine this definition point by point.

"Inconsolable crying." This is probably the aspect of colic which distresses parents most. Most young infants can be quieted with holding, walking, a pacifier, a car ride, a feeding, quiet talking, etc. Colicky babies, by contrast, are for long stretches simply beyond help. Parental intervention seems to have no effect, or only a temporary one. That colicky babies cannot be consoled is a significant factor which, as we will see later, offers some clues to the nature of colic.

"No physical cause." Colic occurs only among healthy infants. If there is a medical problem which might be causing the baby discomfort, her crying is not colic and, of course, she needs medical attention. If something in her environment—temperature, noise, wet diapers, etc.—is causing her to cry, it is easily corrected.

"More than three hours a day." This is an arbitrary figure. In itself, three hours of crying in one day is not unusual. Only if it happens repeatedly might it indicate colic.

"Three days a week." Most colicky babies have good days when they hardly cry at all, sleep through the night, and seem to be "over it." Parents are doubly upset when the fussing starts again. In my experience, colic wanes and returns. Almost never does it follow the same pattern day after day. According to our definition, a baby can experience colic symptoms less than three and a half days a week and still qualify.

"At least three weeks." Colic as we define it is a persistent condition. This does not mean that you must endure three weeks of screaming before you seek help. Just remember that an occasional bad night, even a bad week, are not unusual.

Table 1 fleshes out this definition of colic somewhat.

Is Colic a Disease?

I believe there are degrees of colic. A baby can have crying which is not so severe and still be called "a little bit" colicky. You may have seen a popular child care book which has a chart showing colicky behavior in one column, just plain crying in another. It is supposed to help parents determine if their child is colicky or not. This is misleading. Colic is not an absolute, all-or-nothing proposition. In fact, one researcher, Dr. Joseph Brennemann, wrote that colic is "an almost inevitable occurrence sometime in early infancy. Few infants escape it."

Brennemann is not using the term "colic" the way we do. He is right that all babies have periods of unexplained fussiness. The fussiness which drives parents to distraction and puzzles pediatricians, the condition which I think deserves the name "colic" and merits a book written about it, is that which lasts for several hours a day over the course of several weeks or months. Brennemann does remind us that colic is not some freak condition set apart from normal infant behavior. It is an extreme form of what all babies do. A baby who cries and cries is like a baby who has no hair for a year, or a baby who consistently outperforms all growth charts—unusual, but not abnormal. Colic is an anomaly, *but it is not a disease.*

Table 1

DESCRIPTIONS OF COLIC

COLICKY INFANTS HAVE SPELLS OF:

> Unexplained fussiness, fretfulness, irritability, crying
> Piercing screaming attacks
> Explosive or inconsolable crying
> Noise and rumbling in the gut, excessive flatulence or gas (and/or)
>   apparent abdominal pain with legs drawn up onto the abdomen
> Fists clenched

COLICKY INFANTS ARE:

> Vigorous
> Intense, wound up
> Energetic, excitable
> Easily startled
> Gassy
> Grimacing, stiffening, twisting
> Easily and frequently awakened
> "Squirmy as a worm in hot ashes"

Colic Is Very Common

If your baby has colic, you are not alone. Once you begin talking and asking about it, you will be amazed at the company you are in. Ask your parents, in-laws, aunts and uncles. I guarantee, yours is not the first colicky baby in your family (although colic is not hereditary). Talk to your friends, and you'll find that yours is far from being the only colicky baby in your neighborhood.

One out of five babies has colic. It occurs in all cultures. The Chinese describe what we call colic as "hundred-days-crying," and consider it a normal behavior pattern. The condition has been recorded for hundreds of years. Remember Shakespeare's lines about the seven ages of man: "At first, the infant crying and puking in the nurse's arms." The first pediatrics textbook in English, *The Boke of Chyldren*, refers to "colicke" as "rumbling in the gut." This was in 1553, before the introduction of coffee and tobacco to England (so much for blaming the mother's bad habits for her child's distress). Do not think that our hectic twentieth-century lifestyle is responsible for colic. Colic has been with us as long as there have been babies, and we are only now beginning to understand what it's all about.

The Four Most Important Things to Remember About Colic

My message to parents with colicky babies is simple:

1. *Your baby is healthy and will thrive.*
2. *You are not the cause of your baby's colic; it's not your fault.*
3. *It will pass.*
4. *You can take steps to cope with colic and to make sure that there are no lasting ill effects.*

I urge physicians to repeat this brief litany to parents, and parents to repeat it to themselves, over and over.

Chapter 2

Doctors and Colic

If colic is so common, why doesn't it get more publicity? Judging from the dearth of information on colic you would never guess that it affects over 20 percent of all babies born. That's over seven hundred thousand infants each year in the United States alone. It is a large-scale problem. Yet this is, I believe, the first book which fully discusses the colic mystery.

I have worked with many parents of colicky infants. They have helped me see that colic is one of the "dirty little secrets" of pediatrics. Often, parents are made to feel embarrassed about mentioning it. Many pediatricians don't want to hear about it. Your own pediatrician may have said, "Oh, that's just a touch of colic," and left you to cope on your own. Try to understand the reasons for this lack of professional advice.

The Curious History of Colic

Historically, colic has eluded medical understanding. At various times, researchers writing in reputable publications have blamed colic on: overfeeding; underfeeding;

food with too much carbohydrate, too much starch, too much protein; "allergy": a reaction to horsehair, feathers, orange juice; overpermissive parents; too much picking up of the baby; exposure to cold; congenital syphilis; and lack of oral satisfaction, among other causes.

Suggested "cures" have included: weaning the baby from the breast; adding goat's milk, olive oil, or banana powder to her diet; treatment with bicarbonate of soda, chloral hydrate, opium derivatives, peppermint or dill water; giving an enema or suppository; offering a pacifier; handling the baby more gently; and a drink of whiskey. (R. S. Illingworth, a famous British pediatrician, clarifies "taken by the baby.")

I do not want you to think this is unusual. Reviewing the literature on almost any condition gives you a variety of absurd notions that were taken seriously for a time. In the case of colic, however, no cause has been isolated nor a definition agreed upon, so many of these mistaken ideas have hung on. Only in the last thirty years have controlled experiments comparing groups of colicky and noncolicky babies on these and many other points proved definitely that none of these "causes" are to blame and none of these "cures" effective.

Colic Is Not the Sort of Problem Doctors Like

Little is taught about colic in medical schools. It is not the sort of problem doctors feel comfortable with. It is not a disease. It does not have a definite cause. It does not even have a telltale set of symptoms. Nothing about colic shows up on x-rays, stool analyses, blood tests. Diagnosis is subjective. There is no treatment of choice, which, understandably, makes doctors shy away from it.

One thing pediatricians *do* know about colic is that it does not kill or harm infants. They know that the infants will outgrow the problem fairly quickly. What they do not realize is how devastating it is to the parents while it is going on. The physician will frequently say to the mother, "This is not serious. If only you would relax and take it easy, then your baby would calm down." Yet I have given talks on colic to groups of physicians and played for them a tape of a colicky cry. After no more than a minute and a half of this noise, I get cries from the audience: "Enough!" "Turn it off!" Perhaps if pediatricians had to spend even one evening with a colicky patient, they would be more sympathetic.

The Nature of Colic in
Behavioral Research

Another reason for the neglect of colic may lie with the nature of research into human behavior. Some doctors and researchers like to observe children only when awake, while others like to study children asleep. Like larks and owls, these professionals do not flock together—they do not talk to each other or share their findings. Colic, which is a strange sort of condition somewhere between awake and asleep behavior, has fallen into an academic no-man's-land.

There is also a species of researchers I call hawks. Rather than observe, they like to do things to babies and then measure their responses. They snap rubber bands against heels, block the air flow through the nose, make a baby breathe a low oxygen air-gas mixture. Some of these hawks seem truly aggressive; however, they have added greatly to our knowledge of child development. Unfortunately, there is no way for them to provoke or simulate a colic spell in the laboratory. Few researchers care to be out taking measurements in the evening, when most colic occurs. Since every baby is different, and no baby's colic is exactly the same from day to day, controlled experiments are difficult. This is why colic has been described by the larks, but not really studied by the hawks.

In the academic aviary, larks, owls, and hawks live in different trees. These various professionals have their own journals and their own languages. Specific kinds of behaviors are usually studied separately from one another: crying separately from social smiling, night awakenings separately from length of sleep-cycle periods. Yet colic involves many kinds of behaviors. My intent is to explain, in plain English, how seemingly separate infant behaviors might relate to each other: colic, crying, temperament, and sleeping problems. I will suggest that control of breathing during sleep might influence all of these. Colic has not fallen into any discipline's territory so far, but now it may well be in a territory of its own!

A Bias Against Moms?

I believe there is also an element of condescension toward women. When some male physicians see a distraught, tearful, exhausted mother asking for help with her child's colic, they tend to assume the problem lies with her, rather than the child. Even if they admit colic is a pediatric problem, they take an easy out: blame the mother; blame her diet, breast milk, choice of formula, inexperience, her overly active imagination, and so on. In this sense, colic is a little like menstrual cramps: male doctors who've never experienced them assume it is all in the woman's head.

Some doctors are so unwilling to talk seriously about colic that the mother resolves never to bring it up again. Her baby may still cry, but as far as the doctor knows the condition has abated. So the doctors who scoff most at reports of colic often have their mistaken ideas confirmed. Needless to say, you shouldn't pretend to your pediatrician that your baby's colic has gone away if it hasn't. You will be helping him perpetuate his ignorance, and your problem.

What Can a Doctor Do About Colic?

As far as treatment goes, most pediatricians do not believe there is anything they can do. They try to stall and/or reassure the mother until the colic runs its natural course. Some physicians try to treat colic with phenobarbital, herbal teas, or drugs intended to prevent gas formation in the stomach. Even antacids have been used! Other drugs which decrease the muscle tone in the intestines have been prescribed. The decision whether to prescribe drugs depends on the pediatrician's training, whether he or she had children with colic, and the amount of pressure the doctor is getting from the parents to try to stop the screaming.

I am frequently amused when a pediatrician announces that he has "cured" a case of colic. Usually he has had the mother try a series of "treatments" over the course of several months. Then around the child's twelve- or sixteen-week birthday, one teatment has magically worked. Alas, that treatment doesn't work on the next child, or the next, or the next. The point is that the colic cured itself, and would have done so in any event. Mistakenly attributing the cure of colic to that week's treatment has led to no end of unhelpful ideas about how to cure colic. This often happens with conditions that clear up spontaneously. Your doctor may suggest chicken soup for a cold and you may find that after eating chicken soup for six days your cold is gone, but that does not mean that the chicken soup cured your cold.

Until definitive treatments for colic are developed, there is still much a doctor *can* do. He can learn all there is to know about this very common problem. He can make sure the colicky child remains healthy and gains weight properly. He can keep parents from exhausting themselves physically and emotionally over mythical causes and cures. He can offer a sympathetic ear, calm understanding, and sincere interest. A follow-up telephone call to parents asking, "How did things go last night?" can be an invaluable boost to their morale. A doctor should see the mother in person often enough to look for signs of exhaustion, despair or great family stress, and be prepared to recommend help. He should be current on medications for colic, in case drug intervention should become necessary.

You and Your Pediatrician

Do not lose faith in your pediatrician if he or she seems at a loss over your colicky baby. This is a tricky problem which some physicians handle better than others. Your doctor may be splendid about every other aspect of your child's health and development. You may be lucky enough to find someone else—a sympathetic relative, a friend who has been through colic herself, a clinic nurse—to help you through this time. However, if your baby's colic makes your pediatrician impatient, patronizing, or less willing to spend time with you, this may be as good a time as any to find a more sympathetic doctor. Don't simply accept your pediatrician's suggestions regarding switching formulas (see page 24) or hospitalization (see page 124). If such advice is given, ask your baby's doctor: What do you really expect to accomplish by this treatment?

Chapter 3

Eleven Myths About Colic (and Why You Shouldn't Believe Them)

Once friends and relatives hear (or decide) that you have a baby with colic, the advice will start. You will hear all sorts of theories about the causes of colic. People will offer their own pet remedies, and you will probably become very confused.

Here are eleven popular fallacies about colic. They have grown up and gained acceptance partly because colic is different things to different people; since there is no standard definition, the field is wide open. Some of these fallacies are based on observed relationships, one-time coincidences, or simply what seems logical. None of them can stand up to scientific scrutiny. I will explain why you should not believe any of them. Then I hope you will put them out of your mind and devote your energy to coping with your noisy little bundle.

Fallacy #1: There Is No Such Thing as Colic.

Some doctors say they have never seen a colicky baby. They believe the problem is with overanxious, inexperienced mothers who exaggerate normal crying all out of proportion. I would remind these doctors that they seldom see babies in the evening, when colic is usually at its worst. They do not have to listen to hours of crying day after day. Too many mothers—experienced, calm, third- and fourth-time mothers —have reported similar crying patterns for colic to be a fiction.

Fallacy #2: Maternal Anxiety Causes Colic.

No more destructive a belief could be imagined than this one. Imagine telling a mother who is already worried about her child's crying that she is responsible! The guilt, resentment, anger and frustration produced by this fallacy is enormous. It can cause others in the household to blame the mother for the colic. Worse, it can cause the mother to believe it herself.

Believing that colic might be her fault can keep a mother from getting the help she needs. Once she decides that she is less than perfect at mothering, discussing the infant's behavior with her pediatrician or with *anybody* becomes painful.

If a parent believes it is her or his fault that the baby is miserable, every cry becomes an accusation. It would be instructive for someone to study whether colic—and the fallacy that parental inadequacy has caused it—is related to child abuse or other domestic violence. One abusive father I know was untroubled by what he felt was "hunger crying," but became violent at the sound of colicky crying, which he interpreted as disapproval. "The baby was angry at me," he said, and he reacted by striking the infant.

In any event, as you will read in the next chapter, careful studies have shown that mothers of colicky babies are no more anxious, high-strung, or emotionally unstable than the mothers of quiet babies. Parents are *not* responsible for colic.

Fallacy #3: Colic Is a Gastrointestinal Problem.

This may be the most deeply entrenched myth about colic. The term itself comes from "colon," implying some connection with the digestive system. The first English language book on pediatrics, *The Boke of Chyldren,* published over four hundred years ago, described colic as noise and "peine in the gut."

It's not hard to understand where this idea came from. Often in the course of crying spells, infants draw their legs up to their abdomens and pass gas. Colic spells often occur after meals, suggesting something amiss with digestion. Also, colicky crying has been described as waxing and waning, as if waves of colonic spasms were afflicting the infant. (The smooth muscle in the colon does in fact contract in regular waves, thus pushing food and fecal matter through.) Thus, observers through the centuries have made the connection: colic originates in the abdomen. But, as you will read in the next chapter, researchers have tried to prove this theory and come up empty-handed. Illingworth and Jorup used x-rays and barium enemas, and found no special gastrointestinal activity during colic spells.

The colicky behavior which gave rise to this theory—the drawing up of legs, turning red, clenching fists—also occurs, momentarily, whenever an infant gets a baby shot. So it may not indicate pain in the abdomen at all—it may simply be the way a young infant expresses discomfort, from whatever location. As for the gas, I believe that as she cries, an infant swallows air that must then be expelled. It is a result, not a cause, of prolonged crying. Similarly, the waxing and waning feature is probably the way any baby would cry who has been at it for hours.

Most convincing is this: colicky babies do not have any symptoms of intestinal disorders. No poor weight gain, no excessive spitting or vomiting, no constipation or diarrhea, no need for extra feedings. Surely, after all these years of careful study, some physical corroboration for this idea should have shown up. Therefore, there is no reason to believe that colic reflects a gastrointestinal problem.

Fallacy #4: Something the Baby Has Eaten Disagrees with Her.

If you have a food allergy, you might assume that your colicky baby does too. It is true that some children are allergic to the cow's milk protein in some formulas, but this is not colic. Yet a common treatment for colic is switching formulas from those containing cow's milk protein to those derived from goat's milk or soybean protein, or some "hypoallergenic" formulas.

A recently published report claimed to prove that cow's milk protein in infant formulas caused colic. However, serious methodologic errors in that study invalidated the authors' conclusions. For example, there was no randomization in the placement of infants into different study groups. The parents were not "blind," unaware of the changes in the type of formula which they were giving their infants. The investigators never defined what they meant by a "cure." And although they claimed that these colicky infants were allergic to cow's milk, about 50 percent of these so-called allergic babies failed to show symptoms when given cow's milk at three or six months of age! The authors claimed they had "outgrown" the allergy, when in fact they had outgrown the colic.

Those same authors also claimed that when a nursing mother has cow's milk in her diet, the cow's milk protein gets into her breast milk, causing colic in her baby. This study also had serious flaws, for the results were based on only ten infants.

The truth is that there is no well-designed study which shows that the diet of nursing mothers has anything to do with colic.

By contrast, a careful, objective study done in 1981 by Dr. William Liebman at the University of California School of Medicine concluded that cow's milk protein allergy has no significant role in causing infant colic.

A related fallacy is that "allergy" in general causes colic. This dates from a period when allergies had just been discovered and were used as the explanation for nearly every medical problem. This vague concept has no basis in fact and is probably only a smokescreen to hide our lack of information.

Another food-related colic theory is lactose intolerance. Lactose, commonly known as milk sugar, is present in all commercial formulas which contain cow's milk. About 10 percent of white Americans, and a much higher percentage of blacks, suffer from an intolerance to lactose. It may cause abdominal pain, gassiness, and diarrhea, but does it cause colic? Liebman's study evaluated colicky infants for lactose intolerance. He concluded that it does not have a significant role in causing colic. Therefore, prescribing lactose-free formulas or having nursing mothers stop drinking milk simply does not make sense.

Researchers who believe that cow's milk protein allergy or lactose intolerance causes colic have never explained how these offending foods, which are ingested throughout the day, would trigger attacks of screaming only at a particular time: 94 percent of infants with colic suffer their worst spells in the evening hours.

As you can see, the strategy of switching to formulas which are free of cow's milk protein and lactose, such as protein derived from soybeans, makes no sense in the treatment of colic. However, there are enough different brands of formulas so that a pediatrician might suggest a formula switch each week with the idea of buying time until the infant outgrows the colic. This is a deplorable strategy, especially when the doctor should know it will not work. He might think that the mother will feel better if she has something different to try, but, on the contrary, I suspect that this only increases the mother's frustration. As each successive new formula fails (sometimes until the infant is about three months old!), she suspects more and more that something must be dreadfully wrong with her child or with herself.

If your physician suggests switching formulas in an attempt to cure your baby's colic, do not lose patience. Remember that this is a long-standing practice. Ask your pediatrician to discuss frankly whether he or she thinks the treatment will really work, or whether it is designed simply to placate you so that you can feel better.

Fallacy #5: The Nursing Mother's Diet.

Foods that cause stomach upset or gas in the nursing mother go on to cause colic in her baby, right? Wrong! This fanciful notion is contrary to everything we know about how digestion occurs.

The foods eaten by the mother get broken down into simple elemental foodstuffs and absorbed by her digestive system. Breast milk is made from these absorbed nutrients. By contrast, gas in the mother's intestine is formed much further along in the process by the action of naturally occurring bacteria in food the mother has eaten. It is impossible that gas in the mother's colon, derived from eating something like beans or cabbage, could get into her breast milk. Yet some nursing mothers report that eliminating certain foods from their own diets improved their children's behavior. You may have heard some of your friends swear this is true, but it is not. It is only coincidence, or wishful thinking.

Mothers who believe that their breast milk is causing their children's misery must be reassured that it is not, since it may cause mothers to stop nursing when there is no reason to do so. Since nursing is one of the few things that can sometimes soothe a screaming baby, a mother can be filled with conflict over whether it helps or hurts.

A professional woman torn between staying home to nurse and returning to work (and who for some reason will not consider partial nursing) sometimes seizes on her baby's crying to resolve the conflict. A mother should not use the belief that "bad" or insufficient breast milk causes crying as a reason to return to work quickly; it may provide a handy excuse, but it has no basis in fact.

You'll read some practical tips on breastfeeding a colicky baby in Chapter 9. In the meantime, you can be sure that "bad" or insufficient milk has nothing to do with colic.

Fallacy #6: Breastfed Babies
Have Less Colic.

Since there is a prevalent assumption that breastfed infants are healthier in all regards, there also is the assumption that breastfed infants are protected against colic. However, several studies have shown that colic occurs as often for breastfed infants as for bottle-fed infants. Dr. T. C. Boulton's study from the University of Adelaide in 1979 noted that colic was unusually common in Australia (40 percent of all babies), but that it was as common among breastfed as formula-fed infants.

Fallacy #7: Firstborn Children Have
Colic More Often.

Many mothers swear this is so, but why? Firstborn children are a little like a trial cake. Probably out of uncertainty and inexperience, parents regard the first child as more difficult in a number of ways, even though objective ratings of temperament show that firstborn infants are no different from subsequent ones. There is no biological reason why a firstborn child should be more prone to colic, and as for psychological reasons—well, this is just a variation of the maternal anxiety argument.

The study by Dr. Jack Paradise and others has shown clearly that colic occurs as commonly among subsequent infants as among firstborns.

There may be what we call a reporting bias at work here. A mother may simply deny—or refuse to believe herself—that a second, third, or fourth child has colic. If her first child did not have colic, she is perplexed: "It's not supposed to happen this way; I wonder what went wrong." If her first child *did* have colic, she has even stronger emotional reasons for denying that it has happened again. Perhaps she still feels a little guilty about the first case. Perhaps she didn't get satisfaction from her doctor and doesn't see any point in bringing it up this time. Perhaps she feels that two colicky babies are a certain sign of her doing something terribly wrong. What this is, is a certain sign of bad luck, nothing more. Perhaps she is better able to deal with the problem if no label is attached. Careful examination of mothers' reports of crying and fussy behavior in subsequent-born children shows that they are often identical to most definitions of colic.

Then again, some mothers just face it. I had a mother tell me, with a tone in her voice as though she were being punished, "I survived not sleeping for three months with the first two; I guess I can do it again. Anyway, those children are fine now so we'll just wait it out." Try to tell this mother that colic occurs only in firstborn children!

Fallacy #8: Fresh Air Causes Colic.

Several mothers, primarily from rural backgrounds, have told me about "wind colic." The idea here is that taking a baby out in the night air or on a windy day causes cramps and great fussiness the next day. Some of these mothers even warn against leaving the window in a baby's room open at night.

There is a long tradition of believing that "night air" causes all sorts of illnesses, but it is no more true in the case of colic than anything else.

Fallacy #9: Boys Get It More Than Girls.

The only explanation for this fallacy is that mothers might perceive problems in their sons more often than in their daughters, boys being thought more mischievous, stubborn, etc. than girls. At any rate, it is not true. A study by the Canadian pediatrician, Dr. W. C. Taylor, and other studies agree that infant boys and girls share an equal risk in developing colic.

Fallacy #10: Better-Educated Mothers Have More Colicky Babies.

It sounds fanciful, but many people believe that the higher the mother's education level and social class, the more prone to colic her baby is. You will also hear it stated in the contrary way: Colic is less common among families of lower social class status.

These fallacies probably come from the patient selection bias of most pediatric training programs. Pediatric residents often learn from, and practice their skills on, poorer families who do not have private pediatricians. These families tend to visit emergency rooms and clinics sporadically, and often delay seeking medical care. Complaints of colic may be less frequent among these families when compared to middle-class families leisurely discussing infant behavior in their private pediatrician's office. Then again, perhaps better educated mothers read too many child-care books. Perhaps they are too quick to decide that normal crying is colic. Perhaps they are less tolerant of whining and crying.

Careful studies show that social class or maternal education level bears no relationship to colic. While it's true that a recently published study from England suggested that colic occurred more commonly among infants of parents who were in higher social classes, there was no definition of colic stated in that paper. The authors also did not indicate how they asked their questions. For example, parents' responses to the question, "Does your child have colic?" may reflect social group differences in interpreting the term "colic." As part of my own studies I have examined detailed, narrative descriptions of infant behavior and fussy periods. There is no question in my mind that colicky behavior, whether the parents call it colic or something else, occurs equally among all social classes.

Fallacy #11: Colicky Babies Are More Intelligent.

You may hear it said that children with colic are more intelligent than others, or grow up to be more ambitious, driven, persistent, etc. No study has ever supported or refuted this fallacy. Pediatricians generally recognize it as a "white lie" intended to help the parents live through this difficult period.

Here we have eleven common myths about colic laid, I hope, to rest. Believing in or acting on any of these ideas cannot necessarily help you. It can distract, upset and exhaust you. Better to learn what we know for certain about colic, and use this knowledge to act constructively on behalf of your infant, family, and self.

Why So Many Myths?

Why is there so much misinformation about colic around? Partly, as I have said, because of a lack of real factual information—mythology loves a vacuum. Also, the definition of colic has been so vague that people have included only those cases which fit their pet theories and excluded those that don't. Most responsible, I believe, is our human tendency to see cause-and-effect relationships in what are only coincidences. This tendency is particularly frequent in the case of colic, which varies inexplicably from day to day.

Consider these examples: A mother might take her baby out in the cool air one night and the next day he might have an especially bad colic spell; she decides that the night air caused the colic. A breastfeeding mother might stop eating starchy vegetables; the baby may then have a couple of relatively quiet days; she decides that vegetables caused the colic. Perhaps one baby's colic has run its course at the same time his mother switched to a new formula; she may tell all her friends that Formula X causes colic. A person may know three boy babies with colic and no girl babies; he may conclude that boys have more colic than girls.

These are all errors. But you can see how the old wives' tales in this chapter got started, and how they seemed to be "proved" just often enough to keep them alive. While some of the "causes" may seem to explain a small number of cases, and while the "cures" may seem to work for a couple of days, in the long run none of them holds up.

To separate coincidence from demonstrable truth, science has devised rigid procedures for experiments and research studies which can tell us with great reliability what has been true in the past, and what will probably be true in the future. You will read about some important, properly conducted studies on colic in the next chapter.

Chapter 4

What We Actually Know About Colic

What researchers tell us about colic is nowhere near as colorful as what magazines and mothers-in-law tell us, but the former is a lot closer to the truth. I believe that the unromantic facts about colic must be better publicized if parents are to face colic calmly, and if doctors are to move forward in understanding it.

This is not to say that every study by a person with letters after his or her name deserves our attention. Many of the colic myths cited in the last chapter have been started or confirmed by reputable doctors doing, what appeared at the time, to be serious research. In every case, however, we can go back and see that there were flaws in the way the research was conducted. Perhaps the sample size was too small, the definition of colic too vague, the evaluation too subjective. For example, some of these studies depended on parents' recollections of past behavior; these retrospective studies are considered quite unreliable. In other cases, researchers did not protect against their expectations coloring their findings, or failed to use statistical analysis to make sure that the connections they observed could not have occurred by chance alone.

Fortunately, medical research is constantly reevaluated. A new generation of doctors conducts new kinds of experiments, and if these do not back up current beliefs, those beliefs have to change. In this way, older colic research—research which "proves" that diet, inherited allergy, or a neurotic mother is to blame—has by now been pretty well discredited. Unfortunately, the news has not gotten around as well as it should have.

In this chapter I will summarize what I consider to be the key findings of several of the best-conducted colic studies during the past thirty years. Not every point in every one of these papers is equally valid, in my opinion. I have cited here only those findings which have stood the test of time and which I believe are correct. On the whole, each of these studies has contributed importantly to exploding myths and adding to our knowledge of the facts. These are the milestones in our current understanding of what colic is—or, I should say, what colic *is not*.

What Kind of Research?

You may be surprised that so little work has been done on the physiological mechanisms of colic. Most people think that medical research always involves looking inside the body, trying to understand what chain of physiological events —what hormones, chemical changes, electrical impulses, glands, nerves, or organs—can lead to a certain medical condition. Physiological research into something as elusive and self-limiting as colic is almost prohibitively difficult. For instance, most of the usual research tools are inappropriate. No animals appear to suffer from anything like colic; experimenting on rats or monkeys is useless. No child ever died of colic, so autopsies are happily out of the question. Colic is not serious enough to justify anything more intrusive than an occasional blood sample or x-ray. Yet, nothing about colic has ever showed up in blood samples or x-rays—not to mention the fact that patients are only a month or two old, that they are not hospitalized and that their parents do not want to cause them any additional distress.

So you can see that until more subtle experimental procedures are developed and more frequent experiments conducted, we cannot learn about the actual organic mechanisms of colic. And until we understand at least some of the physiology behind colic, we will probably not be able to predict, prevent, and cure it very well. There is some irony in the condition of colic; if it were a graver condition, we would know more about it, and most likely be closer to a treatment.

With what I might call "internal work" on colic so difficult, most studies approach it from the outside instead. That is to say, researchers observe a large number of babies with colic and try to see what they have in common. This allows for generalization about incidence and the usual course of colic. The researchers can explore links between colic and other physical, environmental or temperamental variables. They compare colicky babies with non-colicky babies to see if there are any significant differences between the groups which might explain why one group cries a lot and the other doesn't. This kind of research work asks things like: Does colic often appear to correlate with a history of allergy in the family? Do boys seem to get colic more often than girls? Do babies with colic have, on average, more frequent bowel movements than babies without colic? Questions like these can be answered without doing anything more to the baby than making his mother answer a lot of questions, and as we saw in the last chapter, if the study is not well designed, only serve to generate more fallacies.

Research like this will not give us a cure tomorrow but it is very valuable. First, it can define the usual course of colic, to reassure parents that their baby is neither unusual nor very ill. Second, it can help us deal with colic even before we understand it. Knowing that it is a futile exercise to have the mother keep changing her diet, for example, is certainly worthwhile. Third, correlative research can give important clues toward possible physiological explanations. If, for example, it were found that colicky babies often grow up to suffer from asthma (they don't; this is a hypothetical example), then doctors would know to start concentrating on the respiratory system in looking for the mechanism of colic.

All of the studies below fall into the category of quantitative research. Most began as attempts to prove or disprove some commonly held beliefs about colic. As you will see, the common beliefs almost always ended up being disproved. However, everything we can rule out as *not* being related to colic brings us closer to understanding what *is* related to colic, and what we can do about it.

Dr. Illingworth: It's Not Allergy, Gas or Spoiling

The modern age of colic study dates from 1954, when Dr. R. S. Illingworth published his paper "Three Months' Colic." Dr. Illingworth, an English pediatrician who wrote several popular and influential books on child care, is a British equivalent to our Dr. Spock.

Dr. Illingworth's landmark paper includes an exhaustive, and frequently humorous, review of the medical literature on colic up until that time. He summarizes the assertions of some forty papers in many languages, detailing their contradictory and far-fetched theories on the causes and treatment of colic. (I have borrowed from this review in Chapter 2.) He found that the most persistent theories involved underfeeding, overfeeding, allergy, flatulence and spoiling, among others.

In order to get a base of factual information to prove or disprove these theories, Dr. Illingworth performed a careful study of his own. At the Jessop Hospital for Women in Sheffield, England, he studied fifty colicky babies under three months old whose behavior could best be summed up by the following definition: ". . . said by their mothers to have violent, rhythmical screaming attacks, which did not stop when they were picked up, and for which no cause, such as underfeeding, could be found."

About 20 percent of the babies the doctor saw in the clinic fit this definition. Every time he found a baby with colic, he enlisted the next baby to come in to the clinic, provided that baby had no excessive crying, as part of a control group. In this way, he had two randomly chosen groups of fifty babies each, more or less identical except for the colic, which he could compare.

Dr. Illingworth saw all one hundred babies personally and followed up on them for six months. He collected a great deal of data about them, and their families. Most information, by necessity, came from reports by the mothers and not from his direct observation.

Dr. Illingworth was able to report these data: forty-four of the fifty had developed colic during the first two weeks of life. In all fifty, colic spells always occurred in the evening; in eight, the spells also occurred at other times but became much worse in the evening. Typically, colic symptoms began between 6:00 P.M. and 9:00 P.M. and lasted from one to six hours. (This reminds me of one father who called his colicky little son Dr. Jekyll and Mr. Hyde: when the sun went down the monster came out!) In many of the babies, feeding eased the symptoms for a brief time. Colic disappeared, on the average, at nine and a half weeks. In twelve weeks 85 percent of the babies were over it; by four months all of them were over it.

Comparing the colicky group to the noncolicky group, Dr. Illingworth concluded that colic did not appear related in any way to the factors which had been suggested:

Underfeeding? The fifty colicky babies gained more weight, on average, than the fifty noncolicky babies. Some of the noncolicky babies who gained weight poorly did no unusual crying, while many of the colicky babies had very good gains.

Overfeeding? "I firmly believe that for practical purposes, over-feeding in a young baby is a myth. It is so rare that one can truthfully say that it practically never occurs," Illingworth wrote.

Allergy? There was as much family history of allergy among the babies in the control group as among the colic group. Only seven of the fifty colic mothers said that their eating certain foods had any bearing on the child's colic, and all named different foods!

Stomach or intestinal problems? To address this crucial old question, Dr. Illingworth x-rayed seven of the colicky babies at the heights of their spells to see if there was excessive gas in their intestines. None showed up. To make sure there was no bias, Dr. Illingworth had these x-rays mixed in with a number of x-rays of noncolicky babies and challenged a disinterested radiologist to pick out the seven that were different. The radiologist could not pick out a single one. Barium enemas were also performed during the colic spells. No malformation, obstruction, or spasms in the intestines were found. Illingworth did caution, however, that seven children constitute too small a sample to yield conclusive results.

A previous study in 1952 by Dr. S. Jorup at the Samaritan Children's Hospital in Stockholm also used x-ray studies obtained during the colicky spells. He also found no increased intestinal gas connected to colic.

As further evidence that digestive problems are not to blame, Dr. Illingworth found that the incidence of vomiting and the frequency of stools were the same for both colicky and noncolicky groups.

As for spoiling as a cause of colic crying, Dr. Illingworth has this to say: "It is difficult to understand why rhythmical attacks of screaming, which do not stop when the baby is picked up and such as only occur with pain, should be ascribed to 'over-permissiveness' on the part of the mother. . . . Any parent who has possessed a child with colic knows that it is the most worrying and disturbing complaint, and that a baby with obvious pain has to be picked up and cuddled."

In addition, factors which might bear on spoiling, such as the age of the mother and whether the baby is her firstborn and whether other children in the family had colic, appeared identical for both the colic group and the control group. In addition to de-flating these five key claims about colic, Dr. Illingworth was able to rule out these other factors:

Table 2

FACTORS RELATING TO INFANTS THAT DO
NOT INFLUENCE COLIC

Age of the mother
Parity of the mother (how many children she has had before)
Maternal illness during pregnancy
Number of fetal hiccups
Family history of allergy
Allergy in infant during the first six months
Sex of baby
Birth weight of baby
Weight gain of infant
Number of feedings per day
Method of feeding (breast versus formula)
Amount of spitting or vomiting
Number of stools per day
Increased muscle tone

In other words, the group of babies with colic showed no more allergy, no difference in the frequency of feedings, didn't have younger or older mothers, etc. than the group of babies without colic.

Dr. Wessel: It's Not Allergy and It's Not The Family

Also in 1954, Dr. Morris A. Wessel and four associates at the Yale University School of Medicine published results of another extensive colic project. They had begun work with a strong suspicion that allergy was responsible for a great deal of what they called "paroxysmal fussing" (colic), and wanted to test this and other hypotheses.

Over the course of several years, a great deal of data had been collected on approximately two hundred mother-infant pairs who had passed through Yale's maternity and early infancy project. Data included prenatal interviews, detailed records of the infant's first week, follow-up reports by pediatricians, plus reports from a social worker and psychologist.

Dr. Wessel and his associates sent a questionnaire about family history of allergy to every mother who had been involved; ninety-eight of the women filled out and returned the questionnaire, which formed the basis for the Wessel study.

Fifty of the ninety-eight infants were judged to be "contented," and forty-eight to be "fussy." Of the forty-eight fussy infants, twenty-five were rated "seriously fussy," or "colicky," according to the following definition: ". . . one who, otherwise healthy and well-fed, had paroxysms of irritability, fussing or crying lasting for a total of more than three hours a day, and occurring on more than three days in any one week . . . Their paroxysms continued to recur for more than three weeks or became so severe that the pediatrician felt that medication was indicated."

There is a built-in problem with this definition: It expands the definition of colic to include the pediatrician's behavior as well as the infant's! Whether or not the doctor feels medication is needed probably has less to do with the baby's condition than with the doctor's own training, tolerance, experiences with colic, and how much pressure he is getting from the parents. The ninety-eight mothers kept detailed diaries of their children's crying patterns, eating habits, bowel movements, weight gain, and general behavior. Thus, Dr. Wessel and associates were able to make many comparisons among the contented babies, the fussy babies and the colicky babies.

The theory about allergy quickly proved invalid. There was as much family history of allergy among the contented infants as among the colicky ones. Likewise, there were no significant differences in type of feeding, weight gain, sex, birth order, family history of colic, and mother's education level. Wessel does speculate that fussiness in general, but not colic in particular, shows some correlation to family tension. But his data cannot clarify whether a tense family causes fussiness or whether a fussy baby causes family tension.

Dr. Wessel's study confirmed many of Dr. Illingworth's findings as listed in Table 2, and adds several more:

Table 3

FACTORS THAT DO NOT RELATE TO COLIC

Educational status of mother
Family history of colic
Family tension

Dr. Paradise: It's Not the Mother's Personality

Directly confronting the question of whether a mother's emotional state contributes to colic, Dr. Jack L. Paradise published an extremely useful study in 1966. It was a prospective study, meaning that information was gathered as the babies developed rather than relying on the parents' recollections, and it used a standardized scale to rate the mother's personality, rather than relying on an interviewer's subjective impressions.

Dr. Paradise had been an assistant at the Rochester (Minn.) Child Health Services. He studied 153 full-term infants who were born at a certain hospital during a certain five-month period. This provided a good random sample because he took every baby and did not have a selection bias. A few of the mothers declined to participate and a few babies got sick and had to be dropped from the study so he ended up reporting on 146 infants out of the initial

153. He interviewed each mother at least once a month for three months. He gathered information about the baby's crying, eating, bowel habits, and the mother's own attitudes. He examined the babies frequently.

Twenty-three percent of the infants turned out to have colic, even if moderately:

> unexplained episodes of sustained crying of moderate severity occurring often enough to be considered troublesome or distressing; holding or rocking resulted only in partial or inconsistent relief

or severely:

> prolonged and intense periods of crying or screaming throughout the first three months or longer, not lessened by any attempted method of control, and of overriding concern to the mother.

As you see, Dr. Paradise has brought the reaction of the mother into the equation along with the infant's behavior and the pediatrician's behavior. He has also used terms such as "sustained crying," "moderate severity," and "intense crying" without explanation or further definition. Any observer of infant behavior knows how hard it is to determine whether crying is "moderate" or "severe." And of course what causes "overriding concern" to one mother may not greatly disturb another.

Despite these limitations, Dr. Paradise's study is important because of the way he evaluated the mothers' personalities. He had each of the 146 women complete the Minnesota Multiphasic Personality Inventory (MMPI), a widely accepted measure of personality characteristics. The MMPI includes 500 questions and a number of scales designed to correct for distortions that might be caused by illiteracy, defensiveness, or lying. It is a subtle and proven test which has been used on so many people that there is a large data base with which the mothers could be compared.

With MMPI results (computer-scored) in hand, Dr. Paradise looked for signs of those emotional disorders which previous studies had found connected with colic: overall psychological disorder, anxiety, "rejection of the female or maternal role," and lack of energy or enthusiasm. For each of these, he took the mothers who scored the highest (for example, the most anxious) and those who scored lowest (least anxious), and found that colic was equally common among the children of both groups. He was thus able to eliminate all of these personality disorders as connected in any way with colic:

> The occurrence of colic showed no relationship to maternal emotional factors, whether estimated clinically or measured by a standardized psychological test. Most mothers of infants with colic were stable, cheerful, and feminine. This evidence . . . does not support the frequently stated view that colic results from an unfavorable emotional climate created by an inexperienced, anxious, hostile, or unmotherly mother. By so advising parents, physicians may relieve them of unwarranted self-blame and anxiety.

Dr. Paradise's study also covered some of the same ground as Illingworth and Wessel, confirming their findings. To the list of factors unrelated to colic, he added:

Table 4

FACTORS THAT DO NOT RELATE TO COLIC

Amount of constipation, diarrhea, or flatulence
Type of formula
Duration of each feeding
Father's occupatiom
Maternal intelligence
Family history of gastrointestinal problems
Birth order of infant

Dr. Schnall and Dr. Shaver: It's Not Anxiety

Two subsequent studies have used objective psychological ratings to analyze whether there is a connection between a mother's emotional state and her child's colic.

Dr. R. Schnall and his associates examined thirteen colicky infants who were brought to the Royal Children's Hospital Clinic in

Parkville, Australia. They asked the children's mothers to complete a standardized test called the Eysenk Personality Inventory. As a control group, thirteen noncolicky infants and their mothers were selected, and the same test was used. Dr. Schnall found no more neurosis or anxiety among the mothers of the colicky children than among the mothers of the noncolicky children.

Dr. Benjamin Shaver prefaced his report by reviewing earlier studies which had claimed that colic stemmed from a baby's perception of her mother's anxiety. Dr. Shaver wrote:

> We agree with these authors that babies are exceptionally sensitive to their mother's mood. However, colic rarely begins before the second or third week of life. If colic were due primarily to the mother's mood and level of anxiety, we would expect the symptom to begin in the first few days of life when the mother is the most anxious and unsure of herself. . . . Also, we would expect the first-born of several children to be the most colic prone. This is not the case, however, for ordinal position within the family does not appear to be correlated with development of colic.

With these points in mind, Shaver analyzed a sample of fifty-seven mothers, from the second trimester of pregnancy through the six postpartum months. The babies of twelve of these mothers turned out to have colic (defined by Shaver as "excessive night crying").

To evaluate the mothers' moods, anxiety levels, and adaptation to motherhood, Dr. Schnall chose several characteristics to measure. These included "amount of physical contact," "sensitivity to infant's cues," "sense of humor," and "sense of success as a wife." On all of these items he compared the twelve colic mothers to the other forty-five.

On none of these measures did the mothers of the colicky infants show any differences from the other mothers in terms of personality, or in success at adapting to motherhood. However, Dr. Shaver did find that colic could temporarily disturb the mother-child relationship. The mothers of the colicky babies were less confident and less accepting of their infants when interviewed around the child's three-month birthday. This should not surprise

anyone who has experienced or can imagine three months of
screaming and crying. When Dr. Shaver repeated these measurements at six months—after the colic had passed—the mothers of
the formerly colicky babies were indistinguishable from the control
group: they had gotten their confidence back and accepted their
babies most readily. Apparently mothers are as remarkably
resilient as their suffering babies.

Dr. Carey: Is It Anxiety After All?

Only one contemporary, objective study does claim to find a
link between an anxious mother and colic. This is Dr. William B.
Carey's study of 103 new mothers and their babies. The work was
done between 1965 and 1967.

Dr. Carey interviewed each mother within a few days after
delivery. He used a standardized rating system in which the
mother received a score of 0, 1, or 2 on each of six items: the
woman's relationship with her own mother, her feelings about her
pregnancy, other stresses in her life, etc. Forty of the 103 mothers
expressed some anxiety. Dr. Carey compared their anxiety
ratings with the presence or absence of colic in their children.

He defined colic according to a more rigid variation of the
Wessel definition: crying episodes that were "violent" were
counted toward the more-than-three-hours-a-day criteria. Not
surprisingly, then, he found a somewhat lower incidence of colic
than other researchers—12.6 percent (13 of the 103 infants). Dr.
Carey made the diagnosis of colic or no colic himself.

Dr. Carey reports that only two of the colicky babies came from
anxiety-free mothers, while 11 had mothers in the anxious
category. This is a significant correlation, and justifies Dr. Carey's
conclusion that maternal anxiety appears at least partly responsible for colic.

However, there are a couple of fairly significant flaws in the
research. The first is with his diagnosis of colic. Dr. Carey quotes
and claims to have followed Wessel's definition. However, he
reports that "colic began in the first month for five (infants), the
second month for four, and the third month for four." Wessel's
data, and every other study of colic that I know of, report almost

universal onset of colic within two or three weeks after birth. I have never heard of colic beginning after a baby's first-month birthday, except when the child had been premature. I have no explanation for paroxysmal fussing or crying which begins at two or two and a half months, but I doubt that it is colic. When almost two-thirds of Carey's colicky babies began their fussing after a full month of life, we have to wonder at his diagnoses. Also, as Carey himself admits, he did both the interviewing of the mothers and the diagnosing of their babies. This means the study was not "blinded"; what a mother had told Carey about her anxiety could have colored his view of whether or not her baby's crying ought to be considered colic.

Carey's thoughtful article does temper his conclusions somewhat. He admits that anxiety cannot be the only, or even the most important, factor behind colic. In his sample, most anxious mothers did not have colicky babies and at least two nonanxious mothers did. I believe that, while the question is not closed, the weight of evidence is that the mother's or father's behavior does not cause colic.

Dr. Weissbluth: The Sleep Connection

At the Children's Memorial Hospital in Chicago in 1982, my colleagues and I did our own study of colic. We looked at many of the factors in Tables 2, 3, and 4, but we concentrated on possible relationships between colic and sleep patterns.

Five pediatricians cooperated in our study. They asked the parents of the patients, aged four to eight months, to complete our written questionnaire about their children's sleep patterns. The questions covered the time the child usually fell asleep, when he woke up in the morning, how often he awoke at night, and whether or not the child had had colic.

We received 202 questionnaires and after excluding children with medical problems that might have affected their sleep patterns, we ended up with a sample of 141. Twenty percent of them had suffered from colic (as defined by Wessel).

We found that the following can be added to the list of factors which do not relate to colic:

Table 5

FACTORS THAT DO NOT RELATE TO COLIC

Hour asleep and hour awake
Duration of night awakenings
Parents' attempt to maintain regular sleep schedules
Parents' willingness to allow infant to cry himself to sleep
Consistency and promptness of parents' reaction when infant
    awakened at night and cried
Maternal prenatal smoking or caffeine consumption

However, we did find one significant difference between the babies who had been colicky and those who had not. Infants who had had colic awoke at night far more frequently than the others. They also tended to sleep less in total and to require more time to fall asleep. Remember that this is well after the colic symptoms had disappeared. You will read more about the relationship between colic and sleeping problems in later chapters.

The State of the Art of Colic

As you can see, we know much more about what colic is *not,* than what it is. It is a poorly understood complaint, minor but quite distressing. Studying colic is complicated, and in fact most research has been done around the edges of colic rather than at its core cause.

All studies agree on some things. Colic occurs in about 20 percent of all babies. These babies experience periods of explosive, inconsolable crying with the appearance of abdominal pain and gassiness. The outbursts of unmanageable and disagreeable behavior usually start during the first two weeks, occur mainly in the evening, and typically disappear by three to five months of age. The cause of colic is unknown, but factors such as birth order, sex, parental social class, allergy, maternal intelligence and maternal personality have not proven to be involved.

The one area where some controversy remains is whether a mother's anxiety or general tension in the family plays some role in causing colic. Opinion is strong, but not unanimous, that it does not.

It seems to me that any researcher who seriously maintains that colic is caused by the mother will have to explain three interesting facts. First, why does colic nearly always begin within two to three weeks of birth in full-term babies, and within two to three weeks of *expected* birth date in premature babies? Even if you maintain that the child has to be with the mother (outside of the womb) a few weeks to feel the full burden of her anxiety, why would a premature baby not fuss until she has been living with her mother six, seven, or eight weeks? Second, why isn't colic confined to, or at least much more common among firstborn babies? Mothers are demonstrably more anxious around their first infant, but all studies agree that colic occurs as often among subsequent children as among firstborns. Third, why is colic almost universally worse in the late afternoon and evening? A mother's anxiety follows no daily pattern; why should a child's response follow one? Some doctors have suggested that a mother is more fatigued as the day goes on, or becomes anxious over the father's return home from work. Frankly, mothers of colicky infants are fatigued and anxious all the time. Even when an infant's "day" runs from one in the afternoon to midnight, even when the mother works outside the home and does not see the baby until evening, even when the father works the night shift, colic stubbornly worsens at 6:00 P.M. or 7:00 P.M. no matter what.

I believe that these three facts point to a physiological rather than an environmental cause for colic. I believe that a maternal anxiety explanation simply leaves too many questions unanswered. I want doctors and parents to know that tension in the family is simply not the answer to what causes colic.

Review *all* of the factors listed in Tables 2, 3, 4, and 5. These are things we can say with confidence do *not* have any direct connection with colic. So if you fear that your own anxiety, or your husband's allergies, or your smoking or breast milk or level of education, or your fondness for lima beans is causing your child's misery—reassure yourself. We do not understand the causes of colic, but I am absolutely assured that it is not the parents' fault.

Chapter 5

Crying and Colic

Some of the things we know about crying in general shed some light on colic. This information is helpful to parents who are distressed by their child's crying, even though they might not be facing a full-fledged case of colic.

Parents often ask me why their babies cry at such inconvenient hours! In truth, these nighttime crybabies also cry during the day when such crying is less bothersome and makes less of an impression. When discussing your baby's crying, tell your pediatrician about the "good" times too. Become sensitive to the fact that there are *gradations* between the best and worst of crying times. It might be worthwhile to keep a detailed diary so that you can separate the observations from your perceptions.

It is hard to be objective about crying. Crying is an irritating sound. It seems to bespeak misery and pain. It is impossible to ignore. There is something about it that "poisons the atmosphere," as one mother put it. You can't sleep, enjoy a meal, or concentrate on something else while you can hear your baby crying. This is considered a survival mechanism that must have developed during our evolution. It must be nature's way of making sure your baby gets attention when he needs it.

What Does Crying Mean?

Since crying is one of the few ways a newborn infant can communicate, it is open to interpretation. We may think that a crying baby is hurting, or frightened or angry, or it can be taken as criticism, loneliness or tension.

Tennyson wrote in "In Memoriam":

> But what am I?
> An infant crying in the night;
> An infant crying for the light;
> And with no language but a cry.

There's something in all of us that identifies with a crying baby. Who hasn't felt alone in a strange world, cold, confused, and unable to communicate? We project onto a sobbing child all the despair of our human condition. But I think it is important to realize that we really don't know what a baby's crying means. Although babies do cry when they have been hurt or had a fright, it is not right to assume that a baby is hurting or scared whenever he cries. We don't even know for sure that a crying baby is unhappy. Perhaps the folk wisdom is right that says babies cry "to exercise their lungs," or simply because it's one of the few things they know how to do.

Above all, remember that a screaming infant—colicky or not—is not "doing a number" on you. Infants do not cry to manipulate, punish, or annoy you. They do not know yet that their crying can get results. They do not even know that they are a separate person from you. They are just crying. Perhaps they know why they are crying even less than you do.

What Should Parents Do About Crying?

Illingworth noted that one cause of crying is fatigue. This might suggest that you should leave a tired baby alone to cry himself to sleep. But Illingworth categorically states that during the first few weeks of life an infant should be consoled rather than left alone. He claimed that picking up a baby when he or she cries will result in less crying later on. This has been verified by the direct observational study by Silvia Bell and Mary Ainsworth at Johns Hopkins University in 1972. They disproved the notion that always responding to an infant's cry will encourage crying behavior.

You Can't Spoil Your Newborn

Bell and Ainsworth focused on twenty-six white, middle-class, infant-mother pairs. Data was gathered by observing these mothers and children at home. The observers confirmed first of all that all infants have some crying spells. They noted the number of crying episodes that a mother ignored, the number she responded to, the length of time it took her to respond, what kind of response she made, how effective it was, and the overall effectiveness of the mother in making the baby stop crying. Picking up a baby and holding him proved to be the most effective way of terminating crying. Talking to him or gesturing at him from a distance was the least effective.

Bell and Ainsworth observed that some mothers were deliberately unresponsive when the baby cried, for fear they might spoil the baby. However, data from the study showed the contrary: mothers who consistently and promptly responded to their infants' crying were rewarded with infants who at the age of one year cried less frequently, and for shorter durations, than those infants whose mothers ignored crying, or who delayed a long time in responding.

The authors of that study concluded that infant crying is so disagreeable or "changeworthy" to adults that it probably serves a useful biologic function. They think that infant crying should be viewed as an *"attachment behavior"* or *"proximity promoting"* behavior because it serves to bring the mother closer to the child. Mothers cannot ignore their baby's crying. The Bell and Ainsworth study showed that a mother should not struggle to overcome the natural impulse to comfort her crying child. An infant under three months of age, it appears, is at no risk of being spoiled.

This bears out many studies of infants which suggest that conditioning or training a very young baby is very difficult, even in a carefully controlled laboratory environment. Spoiling, after all, is simply teaching undesirable behavior. Babies under a few months of age maybe cannot "learn" a crying habit because they are not neurologically mature enough. Remember, a baby is not neurologically mature enough at three weeks of age to learn to smile specifically at her mother. Specific social smiling at parents naturally develops at about age six weeks (in prematures, this occurs at about six weeks after the expected date of delivery). If you cannot teach a baby to smile before she is neurologically ready, why assume you can teach her to cry?

Frequent and Infrequent Criers

Bell and Ainsworth also observed that the frequency of crying showed "individual stability" between nine and twelve months of age. Babies under nine months of age did not show much of a pattern regarding frequency or duration of crying spells, but after nine months a baby could be identified as a frequent or infrequent crier, and this identification proved to hold true as the child grew older. We can infer that infrequent criers were those whose mothers had always responded promptly in the early months.

Other studies confirmed that the frequency of spontaneous crying spells is a relatively stable individual characteristic after nine months of age (one even claimed that stability developed earlier—between three and nine months of age). One study induced crying by using a trigger which snapped a rubber band against the foot of an infant, and used the results to argue against individual stability of crying. The relevance of that study to any real-life situation is questionable. However, induced crying and spontaneous crying are similar in that both induced and spontaneous crying tend to decline at about three months of age in all infants.

Similarities Between Colic and Normal Crying

Several studies of normal crying show that the line between normal crying and what we call "colic" is often indistinct. In five fundamental ways, normal crying mimics the patterns associated with colic.

1. *All Babies Cry Some of theTime.*

Crying in infants was first intensively studied in 1945 by a group of dedicated researchers at the Mayo Clinic. In their first study, they observed seventy-two babies in a newborn nursery. They worked in shifts so that each baby was observed twenty-four hours a day. The observers recorded the onset of crying and how long it lasted. They tried to attribute a cause to the crying—wet or soiled diapers, hunger, cramped positions, chilling and the like—if one was apparent. They found that most of the newborns cried between one and eleven minutes per hour. The average daily total duration of crying was about two hours for these seventy-two babies.

Continuous observations were made, and this daily total figure was achieved by calculating fifty of the original seventy-two babies staying in the nursery for eight days—the recommended stay at that time. Remember, these babies were being observed every minute during those eight days. Researchers found that the minimum amount of crying per day was 48 minutes; the maximum amount 243 minutes. All of the infants cried some of the time—at least 48 minutes per day. The average duration of crying was, as before, about two hours per day.

2. *Some Crying Can't Be Attributed to an Obvious Cause.*

The researchers attempted to classify the causes of crying: hunger, vomiting, wet or soiled diapers, and unknown reasons. For example, if the baby was crying and sucking around feeding time, and was calmed by feeding, then the crying was attributed to hunger. They found that hunger appeared to cause 36 percent of all time spent crying. Wet diapers caused about 21 percent of crying time and soiled diapers about 8 percent. Specifically interesting was that 35 percent of all crying was due to "unknown reasons." The researchers were surprised that such a large part of crying—over one-third—could not be explained by any obvious causes.

Then they examined the number of separate crying spells. Each spell was counted once, regardless of its duration. They found that the number of spells for "unknown reasons" were greater than any other cause, including hunger. Their conclusion: crying spells caused by hunger were slightly longer in duration, though less frequent, than those caused by "unknown reasons."

The findings of the Mayo study, then, were that all babies cry during the newborn period and that much of this crying cannot be attributed to any obvious cause. The authors made some guesses about nonobvious causes: bright lights, peristaltic movements or contractions in the gut, loud noises, loss of equilibrium. They added, almost as an afterthought, that perhaps the infants' crying expressed a need for fondling or rhythmic motion.

The authors continued the study on forty-two infants, using a detailed diary filled in by the mothers at home. This data covered about twenty-one days at home, after a nine- or ten-day stay in the nursery. The babies averaged four crying spells a day. *All* babies had some crying spells. Fifty-five percent of these spells were attributed to hunger. Crying associated with vomiting, stooling, urination, overheating, bathing, chilling, lights or noises (the mothers making these attributions) were individually less common than crying for unknown reasons (20 percent). Again, *unknown reasons seemed to be second only to hunger as a cause of crying.*

3. *Two to Three Hours' Crying Per Day Is Average.*

The well-known Cambridge pediatrician T. Berry Brazelton performed an important study on crying in 1962. He utilized diaries completed by parents to study crying in eighty infants. Fussy crying spells unrelated to hunger or to wet or soiled diapers occurred in virtually all the babies. Only twelve of the eighty fussed less than one and a half hours per day. About half cried for about two hours per day. This increased to an average of about three hours per day at age six weeks. Thereafter the amount of crying declined to about one hour per day by age twelve weeks.

4. *Many Babies Have Evening Crying Spells.*

Brazelton also found that crying spells became much more focused or concentrated in the evening by the time the infants were about six weeks of age. By this time, very little crying occurred during the day. The spells of crying in the evening proved to be predictable and began suddenly. The reason for this rapid shift in behavior from a calm/quiet state to a crying state is not known.

This bears out an unpublished study by Dr. James A. Kleeman and Dr. John C. Cobb which said that of seventy-eight mothers questioned about their infants, sixty-eight reported "fussy periods," fifty of whom said that the periods occurred in the late afternoon or evening, and the fussiest hours were between 7:00 P.M. and 9:00 P.M.

5. *Crying Decreases at About Three Months.*

Brazelton found that, on average, crying decreased to about one hour per day by age twelve weeks. Another Harvard study verified Dr. Brazelton's observations using tape recordings of infants crying in their homes. They observed the same time course: an increase in crying at about six weeks, and a decrease by about twelve weeks. Although the amount of daily crying was less than that observed by Brazelton, this may be because only ten infants were studied. This means that the natural history of unexplained crying runs the same time course as that of colicky behavior. In both cases, babies calmed down at about three months of age. Also at this time a stable individual pattern of crying behavior, which will hold true for at least the next year, seems to develop.

Colic May Just Be a Lot of Normal Crying

You can see that, in at least five important particulars, what we have been calling "colic" is just an extreme form of normal crying. Brazelton suggested that those infants in his study who cried more than the others were indistinguishable from infants with colic. I think this is a very plausible suggestion. There is not a great gulf between normal crying and colic. The idea that colic is an all-or-nothing event (like pregnancy) is probably wrong. Colicky babies cry like other babies, only more so. Or, if you prefer, normal babies cry like colicky babies, only less so. The greatest difference between normal crying and colic—amount and day-to-day variation—shows up clearly when crying behavior is put into graph form. Below are charts of three general patterns of infant crying. There are gradations among them, of course, and no baby fits any one pattern perfectly.

Figure 1 shows the most common pattern of "normal" infant crying, including "unexplained fussiness." It should reassure mothers who, noticing that their infant's crying has increased to around three hours a day by six weeks, worry that this increase in crying will continue and turn into colic. This usually never happens. Also, many nursing mothers report "feeding problems" around six weeks. This is also usually the normal peak of unexplained fussiness and has nothing to do with hunger or dehydration.

Figure 2 shows in a general way what colic looks like. As you can see, the onset of prolonged crying occurs shortly after birth. Figure 3 describes infants who, for a few weeks, appear to be developing colic but never actually do. After a few days or several days (not three weeks) of excessive crying they settle down into a pattern resembling Figure 1. Doctors who treat these babies during their fussy first weeks might claim that they have cured colic, but the reduction in crying is spontaneous. It is never appropriate to make a diagnosis of colic until at least three or four weeks of age.

When mothers are allowed to describe their infant's behavior in their own words, several traits become apparent. The descriptions of the colicky period are remarkably consistent. It is impossible to detect differences based on the sex of the child, the social class or age of the mother, or the birth order.

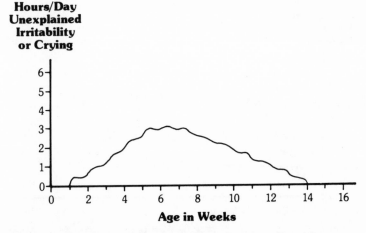

Figure 1. Unexplained fussiness; spares first few days; about two hours/day at two weeks of age; three hours/day at six weeks of age; and one hour/day at twelve weeks of age.

In addition, detailed interviews with hundreds of mothers whose infants had colic, and a study of the diaries they kept of their infant's behavior, makes it clear to me that the salient feature of colicky crying is its erratic pattern from day to day.

Sometimes the colicky crying is rhythmical; sometimes it is a persistent monotone. The crying infant may be easily consoled on one day and absolutely impossible to console the next day. Sometimes infants are consolable in the morning and inconsolable that very same night. Days may occur without any colic spells, and the duration of spells may vary considerably from day to day or within a given day. Nearly all mothers describe rapid and unexplained changes in mood. This seems to be a characteristic of colicky and postcolicky babies. I cannot believe that changes this abrupt would occur unless there were one or several physiological triggering mechanisms.

Is Colic a Different Kind of Crying?

The message of this chapter has been that colic is an unusual amount of normal fussiness. Some researchers and parents object. They say that colicky crying is different from other kinds of crying in quality. Colicky crying, they say, sounds

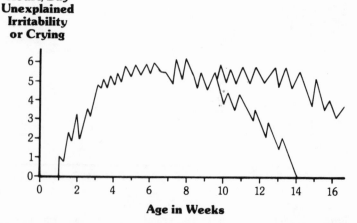

Figure 2. Colic rapidly increases to three or more hours a day with great variation day to day, and might last longer than three months.

different. I agree that a baby in a colic spell sounds different from a baby who has received a shot, for instance. I know that mothers can make even finer distinctions. My wife says that for our four children, the hunger cry was persistent, the tired cry was whining and less forceful, and the colic cry was harsh. Tape recordings reveal that the paroxysmal crying of colicky babies is remarkably similar from one baby to another.

As best I can describe it, colic crying is droning, monotonous, almost mechanical-sounding. It does not have the highs and lows, silences, gasps, moans and sobs of pain crying, or hunger crying. In fact, if we weren't predisposed to call every loud, repetitive, annoying vocalization made by a baby "crying," the noise of colic might have a name of its own. To me, some colic crying is closer to wheezing or gasping than to crying.

Does this mean that colicky babies do something bizarre and abnormal? Not at all. I believe that every baby cries this "gasping" way some of the time. It is simply not listened to carefully or analyzed closely, unless the baby is determined to be colicky. A lot of normal unexplained fussiness probably fits this description. The difference is that it doesn't go on for as long.

We are back to the idea that colic is an abnormally large

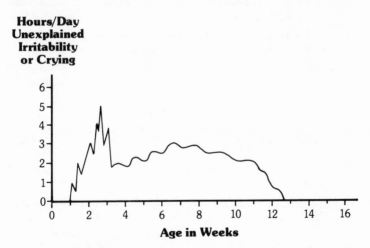

Figure 3. Burst of unexplained fussiness resembling colic, but lasting only a few weeks or only a few days.

amount of normal crying. The question remains, why do some babies get so wound up in their crying that they go on for three, six, twelve hours at a stretch, while most babies cry for only a couple of hours a day?

Which Babies Cry More?

Brazelton suggested that the more "fussy" infants in his study—the ones whom we might call colicky—had a distinct type of personality. They seemed to him more active or sensitive.

Illingworth came to a similar conclusion much earlier. In a 1955 paper called "Crying in Infants and Children," he wrote that the amount of crying for an individual baby is related to the personality of the baby, and that placid and easy babies cry less than determined and difficult babies. He speculated that during the first three months of life, crying is due to loneliness or a desire to be picked up. Perhaps some babies feel this need more acutely, or express it more persistently, than others.

Possibly the difference is physical: something which causes all babies a little distress bothers colicky babies much more. Possibly it is a question of sensitivity: colicky babies are continually disturbed by stimuli which other babies can ignore. Possibly it is a question of temperament: not all babies are able to calm themselves down at the same rate, and seriously colicky babies may be unable to calm themselves down at all. It does seem that babies with colic tend to be more determined, sensitive, and difficult to manage.

You will read more about the temperament connection in the next chapter. In the meantime, remember that your colicky infant is not doing anything that other babies don't do. She is just doing it a little more persistently.

Chapter 6

Infant Temperament and Colic

Some parents can be philosophical about colic. They can say, "Well, he's just that kind of baby." They may be right. There turns out to be a significant association between colic and a certain kind of infant personality. One mother asked me if we could cure her fussy baby by performing a personality transplant!

That babies have personalities is not news. Your baby has an individual style of behavior at a very early age. Some mothers know before delivery that their baby will be unusually active. When babies are only thirty hours old, temperament differences between ethnic groups can be measured. Behavioral differences might reflect inherited or genetic traits. They might also be acquired traits, possibly reflecting environmental influences during pregnancy. Many child development specialists believe that both genetic and environmental factors combine to affect the behavior of newborn infants.

Colicky Personality?

Table 1 described colicky infants as vigorous, intense, energetic. As you read in the last chapter, Dr. Brazelton has called colicky infants active and sensitive. Dr. Jorup in his classic study mentions that colicky babies are excessively sensitive to sound and light, sleep for unusually short periods, and seem restless in general.

What is the truth about colic and a certain kind of temperament? Since temperament is such a subjective factor, could a colic temperament even be measured?

A Standardized Temparament Rating

All parents naturally make their own assessments of their babies' temperaments. You may be surprised to know that there is a standardized system for evaluating infant temperament. It is not absolutely objective, and it has a number of limitations which I will point out later, but it has proved over the years to be very useful and statistically sound.

The researchers who developed this system, Drs. W. B. Carey and S. C. McDevitt, did not have colic anywhere in their minds. There is not even a crying dimension in their system. No one correlated temperament, as rated on this scale, with colic until much later. However, as you will see, the correlation proved to be striking.

Infant Temperament Characteristics

Carey and McDevitt refined their method of measuring infant temperament in 1977. Starting with nine characteristics that had been described earlier by Alexander Thomas and Stella Chess of New York University, Carey and McDevitt developed a parent-response questionnaire that has been widely used around the world. It measures the following:

1. *Activity.*

Does the infant squirm, bounce, or kick while lying awake in a crib? Does she move around when asleep? Does she kick or grab during diapering? Some infants always appear to be active, others only in specific circumstances, such as bathing. I believe activity levels in infants have nothing to do with "hyperactivity" or "laziness" in older children. I have examined a few babies who previously had been referred to a pediatric gastroenterologist because of colic. When he recognized that there were no gastrointestinal problems, he decided that the problem was "hyperactivity." This diagnosis was made on the false notion that wakeful, reactive, or difficult infants are hyperactive. There is no proven association between colic in infancy and hyperactivity when older.

2. Rhythmicity.

Rhythmicity is a measure of how regular or predictable the infant appears. Is there a pattern in the time he is hungry, how much he eats at each feeding, how often bowel movements occur, when he gets sleepy, when he awakens, when he appears most active and when he gets fussy? As infants grow older, they tend to become more regular in their habits. Still, some babies are very predictable at age two months, while other babies seem to be irregular throughout the first year.

3. Approach/Withdrawal.

Approach/withdrawal is a temperament characteristic defining the infant's initial reaction to something new. What does he do when meeting another child or a baby sitter? Does he object to new procedures? Some infants reach out in new circumstances; accept, appear curious, approach; others object, reject, turn away, appear shy or withdraw.

4. Adaptability.

Adaptability is measured by observing such activities as whether the infant accepts nail cutting without protest, accepts bathing without resistance, accepts changes in feeding schedule, accepts strangers within fifteen minutes and accepts new foods.

5. Intensity.

Intensity is the degree of an infant's response, either pleasant or unpleasant. "Intense" infants react loudly with much expression of likes or dislikes. During feeding they are vigorous in accepting or resisting food. They *react* strongly to abrupt exposure to bright lights; they greet a new toy with enthusiastic positive or negative expressions; they display much feeling during bathing, diapering or dressing; and they react strongly to strangers or familiar people. One mother described her colicky baby's intense all-or-nothing reactions: "Her mood changes quickly; she gives no warning —she can go from loud and happy to screaming." Intensity is measured separately from mood.

6. Mood.

If intensity is the degree of response, mood is the direction. It is measured in the same situations described above. Negative mood is the presence of fussy crying behavior or the absence of smiles, laughs, or coos. Positive mood is the absence of fussy crying behavior or the presence of smiles, laughs, or coos. Most intense infants also tend to be more negative in mood than positive.

7. Persistence.

Persistence level, or attention span, is a measure of how long the infant engages in an activity. Parents may value this trait under some circumstances, but not under others. For instance, persistence is desirable when the child is trying to learn something new, like reaching for a rattle, but it is undesirable when the infant persists in throwing food on the floor. Unfortunately, some babies persist in their prolonged crying spells and their prolonged wakeful periods. One father described his persistently crying baby as follows: "We have a copper-top alkaline battery-powered baby and we're powered by regular carbon batteries. He outlasts us every time."

8. Distractability

Distractability describes how easily the baby may be distracted by external events. A distractable infant's sleep or hunger cry is easily consoled by picking up the infant; fussing during a diaper change can be stopped by acting soothing. The infant is easily distracted by new toys or unusual noises. Distractability and persistence are not related to each other, and neither trait is related to activity or threshold levels.

9. Threshold.

Threshold levels measure how stimulus sensitive the infant is in specific circumstances, such as those previously discussed. While some infants are very reactive or responsive to external or environmental changes, other infants barely react.

To determine a temperament profile you would rate your baby one a six-point scale for each of ninety-five questions about his behavior. For example:

	Almost Never	Rarely	Variable Usually Does Not	Variable Usually Does	Frequently	Almost Always
The infant reacts strongly to foods whether positively (smacks lips, laughs, squeals), or negatively (cries)	1	2	3	4	5	6
The infant cries when left to play alone.	1	2	3	4	5	6

(The first question is about *intensity* and the second question is about *mood*.)

"Difficult Temperament"

While observing many children and analyzing many questionnaires, Dr. A. Thomas and Dr. S. Chess (and subsequently Dr. Carey) noticed that some of these temperamental traits tended to cluster together. For example, infants who were extreme or "intense" in their reactions also tended to be slowly adaptable, negative in mood, and withdrawn. This appeared to be a personality type.

According to their parents' descriptions and direct observation by the researchers, these infants seemed more difficult to manage than other infants. Consequently, a child whose scores fall into this pattern is said to have a "difficult" temperament. Some mothers refer to these infants as "mother killers." Infants with the opposite temperamental traits are said to have "easy" temperaments. These are the babies parents dream about having. One father described his "easy" infant as a "low maintenance baby."

Of the original group of infants Thomas and Chess studied, about 10 percent fell into the difficult temperament category. These infants also tended to be irregular in biologic function such as sleep schedules and night awakenings. They were more likely than average to have behavioral problems—particularly sleep disturbances—when they grew older.

One of the most interesting differences between difficult and easy babies is the way they cry when they are past the colicky period. Recently published research found that mothers listening to the taped cries of infants rated difficult (not their own babies), described the crying as more irritable, grating, arousing than the crying of easy infants. They said that the first group sounded spoiled and were crying out of frustration rather than hunger or wet diapers. An audio analysis of the cries helped explain why this should be. The crying of the difficult infants was found to have more silent pauses between crying noises than that of easy babies. Also, at its most intense, the crying of difficult infants was actually pitched at a higher frequency. These two differences can make the crying seem much more frightening, piercing, and annoying.

Why do babies with difficult temperaments cry this way? Do they learn to do it? Is it genetically prewired? Is it connected with other factors which make up a difficult temperament? These are questions which should be explored.

Some professionals contend that the diagnosis of difficult temperament paves the way for future behavioral problems, but in general using infant temperament ratings to predict future development is controversial at best. Many pediatricians have a natural disinclination to label or give undue emphasis to any behavior just because it is at one end or the other of an arbitrary continuum. They also do not like to attach labels which have negative implications. They point out that unusual behavior in adults is accepted as an "idiosyncracy" or "eccentricity" and can in fact indicate intelligence, creativity, or a drive to achieve. Some claim that "undesirable" infant character traits mature into adult virtues. Certainly children with so-called difficult temperaments are every bit as lovable and promising as easy children. They are just a bit more of a handful for their parents. A difficult temperament diagnosis is useful only if it can help parents be prepared and understanding.

Limitations of Temperament Measures

I want to make it clear what the Temperament Profile is, and is not. It is a statistical tool used to describe groups of babies. It is not a very good way to evaluate one specific baby; your own observations are much better. What the Profile does is to put into fairly simple, numerical terms that infinitely complex structure called personality. When done on large numbers of infants, it provides a reliable standard for studies which seek to relate certain factors (in our case, colic) to temperament. But using the results obtained for one infant to make predictions about his or her future is an unsound business. If your child should be given one of these tests, and if you are told the results, remember that it is just a snapshot, and a blurred one at that.

There is a certain built-in limitation to the Profile; ratings cannot be obtained during the first few months of life because the baby does not really show stable behavior patterns yet. This is demonstrated when different rating instruments, The Carey Infant Temperament Questionnaire, the Brazelton Neonatal Assessment Scale, and Bayley Scales of Infant Development, used on the same infant, do not yield internally consistent results. Temperament measures obtained later, at age four to eight months, are moderately stable and can predict temperament measures taken for the next three to seven years.

Interestingly, this development of stability in temperament rating follows a time course parallel to that of crying behavior. After the first few months of life, the amount of crying a baby does—like the temperament traits he shows—develops into enduring characteristics.

Make sure you understand the time frame. When we talk about temperament and colic, we are talking about a baby with colic (before three or four months of age) developing into a baby with a certain kind of temperament (not measured until after four months of age). The two do not coincide.

Another limitation to the Temperament Rating is that the infant does not fill out the questionnaire himself. So the ratings might reflect the preconceptions, and in fact the temperament, of the mother who does the rating. Here we see one of the many built-in quandaries of studying very young children. Unless ingenious tests are devised, everything must be interpreted by an adult. Perhaps it is fitting that this Profile measures both infant behaviors and parental perceptions. After all, how a mother views her infant is probably as important for the mother-child relationship as is how the infant is actually behaving. There is as much a chance of problems developing when a mother merely perceives her infant to be "difficult" as when he is in fact, objectively, a difficult child. Interaction between mother and infant has just started to be seriously studied, but already it is obvious that the infant's behavior, the parents' interpretation of this behavior, and the parents' responses all influence each other in a variety of inter-locking ways. A dramatic example of the difficult child's behavior and parental response spiraling out of control would be child abuse.

A third limitation is that this Profile, like all objective measure-ments, including our definition of colic, uses arbitrary criteria in or-der to put labels on things. But infant behavior is a *continuum*. It has no natural cut-off points. There are some children who are almost but not quite difficult enough in their behavior to earn the label "difficult," just as there are children who cry almost but not quite enough to be diagnosed as "colicky." In addition, if an infant does not rate a difficult temperament, the parents and pediatrician should not assume that all will be rosy.

In spite of these limitations, there is value in using statistical analyses and numerical ratings to identify difficult temperament, and to find relationships between temperament and other dimen-sions of child development.

Difficult Temperament and Colic

It is important to note that an infant's tem-perament does not appear to be associated with the infant's sex, birth order, or social class. It does not seem to be related to a method of feeding (breast or formula) or to birth weight. Curiously, it might be related to ethnic group; one study shows that Chinese infants are more difficult than non-Chinese infants.

Most significant for our purposes, Carey found that *difficult temperament is associated with colic*. He studied a group of infants with colic. Later, when they were old enough to be given the Temperament Profile, four were rated as difficult, four as almost difficult, four as almost easy, and only one as easy. There was, as Carey noted, "a significant concentration in the first two groups."

The association between difficult temperament and colic might have appeared stronger if Carey had included those difficult children who had almost-but-not-quite-enough crying behavior to be called "colicky." Remember, infant behavior is a continuum, while definitions, by their nature, impose arbitrary cut-off points.

Carey's findings do suggest that colic is a combination of excessive but still normal crying plus a perfectly normal temperament, with tendencies toward intense reactions, slow adaptability, negative mood, withdrawal, and irregularity. These many behavioral tendencies which make up difficult temperament, and the crying of colic, may be two facets of the same problem. One may, in some sense, cause the other. They may both have a common cause. Or, as we will explore in the next chapter, there may be a third factor in the equation.

If your baby seems "difficult," whether or not she had colic, hug her, love her, and look forward to the time when she is older. Many parents find that their sour babies really do turn sweet after three or four months. You'll read about some examples in later chapters. There is hope that soon you will all sleep through the night and enjoy your days together as well.

Chapter 7

Is Colic a Sleep Disorder?

I have referred before to an apparent connection between colic and sleeping problems for the baby (that colic can cause sleeping problems for the parents goes without saying). Some researchers have claimed that difficulty falling asleep and frequent night awakenings are an integral part of colic. It has been my experience that sleeping problems may not be apparent while the colic lasts—some colicky babies exhaust themselves crying all evening and sleep soundly through the night—but they often show up later.

Let's review what we know about sleep in general, infant sleep and colicky-infant sleep.

Newborn Sleep Patterns

Normal full-term newborn infants sleep on the average of sixteen or seventeen hours per day during the first three days. Some sleep as little as eleven hours and others as much as twenty-one hours. The longest single sleep period is about four or five hours. However, there is great individual variation in these sleep durations: some infants sleep no longer than 2 hours at a stretch, others sleep up to 10 hours. Decidedly, the type of feeding, breast or formula, and the sex of the infant *does not* influence these sleeping durations.

Infant Sleep Patterns

Over the next sixteen weeks, there are gradual changes in the infant's sleeping pattern. There is a small decrease in the total hours asleep, a doubling of the longest sleep period, and an increase in the amount of sleep occurring at night. By sixteen weeks, most infants are sleeping about thirteen to seventeen hours per day and the longest sleep period is about seven to ten hours. Mothers often start feeding solid food with the hope of getting the child to sleep, but the introduction of solid foods does not alter the development of these sleep patterns. In general, by three to four months of age, most children are sleeping for longer periods of time, and primarily at night. As children become older the total amount they sleep decreases (Table 6).

Your infant sleeps as long as previous generations slept. The age-specific sleep durations shown on Table 6 have not changed over the past sixty years. A study at the Children's Memorial Hospital in 1981 found today's sleep durations consistent with those measured in 1911 and 1927. The social changes in the past sixty years, differences in family size, and how people spend their time, the introduction of central heating and air conditioning, etc., have also not had a signifiant impact on how much children sleep. This would lead us to believe that sleep patterns reflect physiological, genetic behavior as opposed to learned, environmental behavior.

Sleeping Positions

Sleeping position does not affect sleep patterns after the first few days of life. Newborns appear to cry less, move less, and sleep better on their stomachs. However, after a few weeks of age, some babies do sleep better on their backs. In England and China it is customary to place infants on their backs because of the fear that they might bury their head into

TABLE 6

NORMAL SLEEP PATTERN

AGE YEARS	NUMBER OF HOURS ASLEEP FOR 60 PERCENT OF CHILDREN			EVENING HOURS WHEN 90 PERCENT OF CHILDREN FALL ASLEEP
	Nap	Night	Total	
4-11 months	2.0-4.4	9.0-12.5	12.0-16.5	7 P.M.-10 P.M.
1	1.5-3.0	10.5-12.5	12.5-15.0	7-9
2	.5-3.0	10.0-12.0	11.5-14.5	8-10
3	.5-2.5	10.0-12.0	11.0-14.0	8-10
4	0-1.5	10.5-12.5	11.0-13.0	8-10
5	0-1.5	10.5-12.0	10.0-12.5	8-9

TOTAL SLEEP DURATION

6	10.0-12.0	8-9
7	10.0-11.5	8-9
8	10.0-11.5	8-9
9	10.0-11.5	8-9
10	9.5-11.0	8-10
11	9.0-11.0	9-10
12	9.0-11.0	9-10
13	8.5-10.5	9-10
14	7.5-10.0	9-11
15	7.5-10.0	9-11
16	8.5-10.5	9-10

the mattress and suffocate. In the United States it is customary to keep babies on their stomach because of the fear thay they might vomit and choke. These are not reasonable fears; preferred sleeping positions in different countries only reflect different customs. Choose the position that you think is best suited for your baby. We still do not know why some babies sleep better in one position or another.

Understanding Sleep

Studies done in "sleep labs" have helped us to understand some of the mysteries of the state we call sleep. We have learned that the sleep of young infants is different from the sleep of older children in some very suggestive ways.

Sleep States

Sleep is not one constant state. Brain activity during sleep is not static and unvarying, like a TV test pattern. On the contrary, sleep is an active, multileveled, frequently changing condition. There are qualitative differences in sleep patterns throughout the night.

Sleep researchers have identified two basic sleep patterns. The "active" sleep state is called Rapid Eye Movement or REM sleep, because during this state a person's eyes move back and forth rapidly under his closed lids. REM sleep is associated with irregular breathing and heart rhythms and with many fleeting body movements. All dreaming occurs during REM sleep. The opposite state, called non-REM sleep, is associated with decreasing body movements and slow, regular breathing and heart rhythms. The active (REM) and quiet (non-REM) sleep states alternate in a usually predictable fashion throughout the night.

Newborns Have a Unique Sleep Pattern

Researchers have measured the number of REM periods, the duration of each individual REM period, the total duration of all REM periods per twenty-four hours, and the percent of total sleep time spent in REM sleep in subjects of all ages. They have found these measurements basically similar for older infants, children and adults. Only newborns under the age of three months show a different pattern. This means that during the first few months of life, REM sleep patterns may be undergoing organization.

For example, younger infants spend much more time in the REM sleep state that do older children and adults. An infant under three months of age enters a REM state immediately upon falling asleep, while after three months sleep always starts with a non-REM period. Why this is, and why it changes at that age is not known.

Also, the cycle of alternating between the sleep states is much shorter in the infant than in the older child or adult. That is to say, each state lasts a shorter amount of time and one follows the other more quickly. It appears to take about four months to establish the periodic organization of sleep states which will last throughout a lifetime.

Day Sleep vs. Night Sleep

Recent research on infants has focused on differences between daytime and nighttime sleep:

Less REM sleep. During the first three or four months of life, the following rearrangement occurs: REM sleep diminishes significantly during the day, as the number of daytime REM periods decreases, though the length of each stays about the same.

More non-REM sleep. At the same time, non-REM sleep increases during the night as the duration of each non-REM period increases significantly, though the number stays the same.

Fewer REM periods and longer non-REM periods. In other words, something in a baby's nervous system causes a *decrease* in the *number* of REM sleep periods during the day and an *increase* in the *duration* of non-REM sleep periods during the night (Table 7). This may reflect what people mean when they say a baby has to learn to tell day from night, or to "get its best sleep during the night." Clearly there is a lot of behind-the-scenes activity. For little babies each twenty-four-hour period is divided into REM sleep, non-REM sleep, wakefulness, and something called ambiguous sleep because it looks a little like both REM and non-REM sleep.

Table 7

CHANGES IN SLEEP PATTERNS FROM 0-3 MONTHS

	DAY SLEEP (NAPS) 8:00 AM-8:00 PM	NIGHT SLEEP 8:00 PM-8:00 AM	TOTAL SLEEP
REM Sleep	Fewer REM periods (no change in duration)	No change in number or duration	Less REM sleep
Non-REM Sleep	No change in number or duration	Longer duration of non-REM periods (no change in number)	More non-REM sleep

Possibility #1: Colic Is Disorganized Sleep

Not all babies get their sleep organized at the same rate. Let's consider some of the possibilities for a two-month-old baby. Sleep organization may have developed normally, with increasing long phases of non-REM sleep mainly at night. Or sleep organization might be delayed or abnormal, in which case we might see either too many REM periods, REM periods which are too long, or REM periods occurring at the wrong time. Sleep patterns can be disorganized either in terms of the number, duration, or timing of the sleep states.

We do not know what it is in the baby's brain that orchestrates harmonious sleep patterns, nor do we know the effects of abnormal sleep patterns. Perhaps colic results from disorganized sleep patterns, or sleep patterns which are desynchronized with other vital functions such as breathing control.

Sleep and Breathing Rhythms

Some infants may develop the ability to sleep for long periods of time before they acquire the ability to control their breathing during these prolonged sleep periods, or during specific sleep states. The rate of breathing is a relatively stable individual characteristic—some infants tend to be fast breathers and some tend to be slow breathers. However, the rate of breathing during sleep is related to the specific sleep state: people always breathe faster during active sleep states and less fast during quiet sleep states. This relationship between sleep state and breathing rate develops during the first few months of life.

It is possible that some babies have to cope with more asynchrony than others. These babies might not be able to breathe regularly enough to keep themselves asleep. They may sometimes have to fight for air. What better way for a baby to keep her lungs inflated and get plenty of oxygen into her bloodstream than through several hours of lusty screaming?

Charles Darwin, in his book *Expression of the Emotions in Men and Animals,* was the first to point out the important breath-control component in crying. He described in great detail how during crying the arrangement of the facial muscles, gasping sounds, lingering shudders, the way the nose clogs and the eyes close, can all be traced to changes in respiration. Crying, we might conclude, is a strange, overwrought kind of breathing. Remember, in the last chapter we speculated that colic paroxysms might be more like breathless gasping than adult grief- or pain-related crying. It is not too much of a leap to suggest that when breathing becomes disordered because of a lack of coordination with the sleep cycles, the infant might compensate with spells of agitated persistent crying we are calling colic.

I believe that the sleep-breathing-crying connection might hold an answer not only to the puzzle of colic, but to the tragedy of Crib Death or Sudden Infant Death Syndrome. That, too, might be some sort of sleep-related breathing disorder. It is, I believe, significant that when babies are having colicky spells, they are almost never SIDS victims.

Sleep, Temperature and Endocrine Rhythms

If a sleep cycle which is not yet synchronized with breathing could cause an infant distress and lead to colic, a sleep cycle not synchronized with temperature or hormone rhythms could have the same effect.

Body temperatures and the levels of certain hormones go through predictable, daily ups and downs. These rhythms develop during the first year of life. It used to be thought that they did not reach stable daily patterns until after the first birthday. During the first few months especially, temperature and hormone variations are quite irregular, but we now know that serum cortisol (a hormone from the adrenal gland) concentrates in the blood, shows a distinct twenty-four-hour pattern at about six months of age.

Also in newborns, human growth hormone is secreted throughout a twenty-four-hour period. By four months of age the pattern of secretion becomes organized into a circadian pattern. This is, during every twenty-four-hour period there are dramatic differences between the highest and lowest hormone levels, and these peaks and valleys occur at about the same clock hour every day. Once the pattern is established, the hormone is released at night after the beginning of sleep, and the most of the hormone is released during the deeper, later stages of sleep. We do not understand the chemical machinery which links sleep rhythms to endocrine rhythms, but these rhythms might offer a key to understanding colic, especially why colic so often occurs in the late afternoon or evening hours.

Many people, including Dr. Brazelton, explain "evening" colic by saying that the child senses the mother's increasing eagerness/anxiety as the time comes for the father to return home. I think this is an ingenious but unfounded suggestion. Much more plausible is that the occurrence of most colicky spells in the evening is related or linked to distorted biological rhythms.

Is colic infant jet lag syndrome? Biological rhythms which are out of synchrony cause us to feel slightly sick, and jet lag syndrome in adults is an example of this. With jet lag syndrome, we may feel awake, alert, attentive but have difficulty in thinking, focusing, or concentrating. Sometimes we ache or feel worn down, but we still can have difficulty in falling asleep.

So here is one possible line of inquiry that would link sleep with colic: asynchrony between sleep-wake rhythms, temperature/hormone rhythms, or breathing rhythms may individually or together cause distress in an infant. The more disorganized these rhythms are the more severe the colicky behavior. Then, at three months or so, when the transition to a normal, adult sleep-cycle pattern is complete, the colic may disappear, but not necessarily the sleep disorder.

Possibility #2: Colic Is an "Acted-Out" REM Period

Studies in adults suggest that during Rapid Eye Movement sleep, the brain is "awake"—during this time the electroencephalogram superficially resembles alert wakefulness and vivid dreaming occurs—while the body is "paralyzed." This is not paralysis due simply to relaxed muscles. Rather, a neurologically active inhibition of muscles activates during REM sleep.

In a study done on cats during REM sleep, this muscle inhibition was experimentally blocked and the cats behaved as if they were awake. They appeared to be hunting or pouncing on mice while asleep! Perhaps if a similar block was performed on humans (it involves potential permanent brain damage and could never actually be tried), we would appear to act our dreams. One case where we can observe something like this phenomenon in humans is the shaking and jerky movements seen in alcoholics with delirium tremens. This seems to result from an uncoupling between active (REM) sleep and the muscle paralysis that usually goes with it.

Is it possible that the increased motor activity during a colic spell—the twisting, turning, stiffening, clenching—represents a breakthrough in this muscle inhibition? That the baby might be, in a sense, in a state of REM sleep without having yet fully developed the characteristic accompanying muscle paralysis? Typically, a child ends a colic spell by suddenly "falling asleep." This could, in fact, be the onset of a quiet (non-REM) sleep state.

Asleep or Awake?

On the surface, it seems absurd to claim that a screaming, writhing baby is more asleep than awake. But in very young babies, the line between sleep and wakefulness is not all that clear. Often the electroencephalogram cannot distinguish between sleep and wakefulness until at least ten weeks of age. To distinguish between REM and non-REM sleep, measurements of eye and chin muscle activity, or of breathing and heart rhythms, must be taken. It is hard to tell exactly what state an infant is in during a colic spell. Behaviorally, during a colic spell babies appear to be "out of touch," inconsolable, and unreachable. Perhaps they are not really conscious.

If it is true that colic occurs during a Rapid Eye Movement sleep period, then the writhing and screaming might be the behavioral reflection of dramatic shifts in breathing and body temperature which we know occur during REM sleep—shifts we usually don't see acted out because the muscle paralysis keeps the body still.

Indirect evidence suggesting an association between colic and Rapid Eye Movement sleep was published by Dr. Robert Emde at the University of Colorado Medical Center in 1970. In a well-documented series of detailed observations, Dr. Emde noted that infants may appear to be awake—sucking, fussing, crying or smiling—at a time when rapid eye movements are observed under closed eyelids. These "active" behaviors during Rapid Eye Movement sleep tend to disappear by age three months. Over and over again, it appears that the age *three to four months* is a crucial turning point. Although it is only speculation, I suspect that unexplained fussing or colicky behavior in some infants is linked with this crying/Rapid Eye Movement sleep state.

Another study showed that intensive eye movements during sleep, called REM storms, occurred more often in those infants who showed dramatic *"neurobehavioral instability."* That is, these infants showed greater behavioral irregularity, or shifts in behavioral states, from week to week than other infants.

Colic disappears at about age three months. Sleep-state control matures at about age three months. Colic spells almost always terminate with the infant falling asleep. I doubt that all this is coincidence.

With the passage of time, your baby's developing brain becomes better able to inhibit, suppress, turn off, or tune down the ever present background restless, random fidgety behaviors—both when awake and asleep. Also, circadian rhythms develop and become synchronized with each other and day/night schedules. If these are neurologically related events, then both possibility #1 (Colic Is Disorganized Sleep) and #2 (Colic Is an "Acted-Out" REM Period) may be partially correct. The infant with disorganized biological rhythms might have his greatest distress at about the same time every day, and the child who lacks the active inhibitory development appears "wired" or "turned on" during the day and always seems to sleep in an active fashion (uncoupled REM storms?). Colicky babies usually behave as if they suffered from not enough inhibition (too active, too alert), not enough sleep (too wakeful, too fatigued, too cranky), and too much crying at night. Colic appears to be much more of a *neurological* developmental condition than a gastrointestinal problem, *or* a parental problem.

The Crying Temperament — Sleep Connection

We have talked about colic and excessive crying, colic and difficult temperament, colic and disorganized sleep. I believe that the eventual solution to the colic puzzle will draw all of these factors together. For now, I can only suggest where the connections might be made.

Table 8 summarizes a frequently seen relationship between a certain kind of awake behavior and a certain kind of sleep pattern.

Table 8

RELATIONSHIP BETWEEN AWAKE BEHAVIOR
AND SLEEP PATTERN

AWAKE BEHAVIOR	*SLEEP PATTERNS*
Colic	Sleeplessness, "insomnia"
Low sensory threshold	Easily aroused from sleep
Easily startled	Increased frequency of night awakenings
Difficult temperament	Increased frequency of sleep/wake
Increased crying	transition per twenty-four hours
Active, vigorous	

Infant temperament assessments taken between four and eight months, utilizing the questionnaire developed by Carey, showed a clear relationship between difficult temperament and brief sleep durations. Infants with a difficult temperament slept significantly less than infants with an easy temperament. Briefer sleep durations were also observed among infants with colic. It is possible that insufficient sleep causes difficult temperament. Or common factors such as parental behavior and neurologic immaturity could influence both sleep duration and infant temperament.

Several other studies suggest a relationship (as shown in Table 8) between: (1) colic or excessive crying, (2) low sensory threshold, and (3) difficulty in sleeping—either brief sleep durations or frequent night awakenings.

"Low sensory threshold" refers to infants who are easily startled or who respond dramatically to small changes in their environment. In the study which connected temperament and colic, Carey concluded that colic was unusually common among infants who turned out to have difficult temperament and/or low sensory threshold. Sensory threshold is a component of temperament; however, it does not enter into the easy/difficult diagnosis on the Carey assessment. Yet it does prove to have a parallel link to colic. Carey also found that low sensory threshold was associated with frequent night awakenings.

A recent study at the Children's Memorial Hospital tied colic (using Wessel's definition) to a definite increase in the frequency of night awakenings. Older studies have suggested that night waking in children (with or without colic) is associated with brief sleep durations. Night waking also appears to be a problem associated with an abnormal sleep schedule.

Other studies at the Children's Memorial Hospital have showed that babies who are active, intense, and stimulus-sensitive, as determined by the Temperament Questionnaire, have more regular breathing when asleep at night, with fewer respiratory pauses than infants who are inactive, mild, and less responsive to environmental stimulation.

We have a convincing set of linkages here. Clearly, the problems of colic; difficult temperament, low sensory threshold, frequent night awakenings, and brief sleep durations *are* interrelated. Perhaps these are different facets of the same problem. None of them tends to be subject to much parental influence in young infants. None shows much individual stability during the first months of an infant's life. All develop a sharper focus and more enduring pattern after about three months of age. This parallel time course, often occurring in one infant, suggests either that (1) time is required for infants to "learn" behavioral styles and sleep patterns, or (2) some physiological maturing takes place, or (3) both learning and maturing occur.

Support for a physiological view comes from several studies which show that colic occurs in premature infants within a few weeks of the expected birth date, regardless of the gestational age at birth. In other words, colic appears time-locked to biologic development counting from conception, not from birth. Colic most likely has more to do with the physical, rather than the behavioral, maturing of the child.

Colic May Be Part of a Larger Problem

The evidence seems convincing that infants who suffer from colic in their first few months of life have a better-than-average chance of difficult temperament, and/or having sleeping problems later in their infancies. Researchers who feel strongly that colic has *no* aftermath blame this connection on parents. They say that living with a screaming baby for three months causes parents permanently to change their behavior toward the child. They might, for example, become inattentive or "emotionally unavailable" to the child, either out of exhaustion and distress, or as a deliberate management tactic to prevent indulging their baby. It is this parental behavior which, according to this theory, causes behavior problems in the child.

My colleagues and I had a chance to test this theory when we conducted a study of the drug dicyclomine as a treatment for colic. Several previous studies had indicated that dicyclomine can relieve the symptoms of colic. We studied forty-eight colicky infants, some given dicyclomine and some a placebo (plain cherry syrup), and found that dicyclomine is in many cases an effective treatment for colic.

We figured that if dicyclomine eliminated the inconsolable crying of colic, it would also prevent inattentive or emotionally distant parental behaviors described above. If parental behaviors were the problem, we expected to find that infants successfully treated with dicyclomine would emerge from colic with easier temperaments and fewer sleep disturbances than those infants who had received the placebo and kept on crying.

To our surprise, this was not the case. The infants in our study, each diagnosed as having colic (according to Wessel's definition), did show the typical higher incidence of difficult temperament and sleep disturbances as compared to a normal population. But this was equally true of the infants successfully treated with dicyclomine *and* those who had received a placebo. In other words, effective treatment for colic symptoms did not alter later temperament ratings or sleep patterns when the infants were four months old, the assumed postcolic age.

This led us to conclude that difficult temperament and briefer sleep duration in postcolicky infants does not result from the parents' response to colicky crying. Many of the babies in our study had their crying greatly reduced or almost eliminated by the drug, and they still showed a higher-than-average incidence of difficult to manage behaviors and sleep problems.

So it would seem that parents are no more to blame for a four-month-old's brief sleep durations than they were to blame for his crying as a colicky two-month-old. Instead, we believe that colic, difficult temperament, and sleep disorders all share an underlying physical cause. They are all manifestations of the same problem—neurological, respiratory, endocrine and the like. Much more research is needed to determine what is the source of the colic-temperament-sleep triangle, but at least we can feel confident in absolving parents of responsibility for the symptoms.

This does not mean, of course, that your response to your child's behavior has no effect. You can keep a tendency toward difficult temperament from growing into a long-term behavioral problem. You can teach a child with brief sleep durations to sleep longer and more soundly. Your attitude can make colic more or less bearable. The rest of this book is designed to help you learn how to do this.

Chapter 8

More New Ideas About Crybabies

In the past few years, a number of re-searchers have made some bold, fascinating, not-always-reasonable assertions about colic. You may have run across some of these ideas in the medical press or in popular magazines, or you may have heard about them. Let me review the status of some of these new claims.

Naturally Occurring Substances May Cause Colic

A recent study suggests that naturally occurring chemical substances called prostaglandins might cause colic. Prostaglandins are powerful muscle contractors. For example, it is probably prostaglandins that cause contraction of the uterus, and thus the cramps of dysmenorrhea. They might also cause spasm of the smooth muscle in the lung, leading to breathing difficulties. Prostaglandins can similarly contract the muscles lining the intestine.

These chemicals are therapeutically administered to certain infants with birth defects involving the heart. In one study, the authors observed irritability in two infants who had received therapeutic prostaglandins for heart disease. If their observation is confirmed on a larger number of infants, we might be able to conclude that higher levels of prostaglandins—occurring naturally or administered therapeutically—might cause colic.

New research on prostaglandins and similar chemicals has focused on the *unregulated overproduction* or the *unbalanced production* of these substances. We do not yet understand how the tight metabolic control processes work when we are healthy. However, the observations that fatty acids influence the production of these chemicals should lead to exciting research regarding the nutritional composition of breast milk and baby formulas.

Drugs During Labor May Disturb Normal Behavioral Development

Another recently published study, by an Australian physician named Dr. David Thomas, focused on epidural anesthesia during labor as a cause of colic.

Epidural anesthesia does appear to affect both infant behavior and maternal perceptions for a short period after delivery. However, Thomas went much further. He suggested that drugs administered to the laboring mother pass through the placenta so that the baby is born with high drug levels in his blood. The drug levels fall after delivery and, of course, no drug is administered to the infant. So what causes the colic in the infant, Thomas speculates, is in fact drug withdrawal.

In this study, as in the study on prostaglandins, no specific definition of colic was used. In fact, Thomas acknowledged that the assessment of colic is difficult because it can depend on the subjective feelings of the mother and the researcher. Also, the investigator who decided which babies had colic knew ahead of time which mothers had received epidural anesthesia. Preconceived biases might have influenced his diagnoses. The findings in this study would be more convincing if the assessment of which infant had colic had been done in a blind fashion. Due to this flaw in experimental design, Thomas's observations should be confirmed by other studies before we accept his conclusions.

Urinary Tract Infections Cause Colic

The suspicion that colic might be caused by an unrecognized urinary tract infection has generated a lot of speculation. Physicians and parents have spent time waiting to collect urine specimens; infants have endured painful bladder punctures and catheterizations, and infants have been given unnecessary antibiotics. The study which led to this unfortunate state of affairs is called "Colic as the Sole Symptom of Urinary Tract Infection in Infants," a catchy if misleading title.

In this study, again, no real definition of colic was used; only "the appearance of paroxysmal abdominal pain." Only four infants were reported, all of whom were so sick as to require hospitalization (definitions of colic usually state that infants are thriving and gaining weight normally). Moreover, two of the four babies were six months old at the time of the diagnosis of colic. Colic does not occur at the age of six months. Therefore, the concept of urinary tract infections as a *cause* of colic should be critically restudied. Naturally, infants at any age with poor weight gain, fever and chronic irritability should be evaluated for any disease, including urinary tract infections.

Progesterone Level Is Related to Colic

The placenta makes a hormone called progesterone. Generally, the infant is exposed to very high levels of progesterone at birth. A provocative old study, which has been generally ignored, suggests that progesterone deficiency might be a cause of colic.

The authors of that study observed that uterine smooth muscle contractions during labor are accompanied by a fall in the mother's progesterone levels. Those authors wondered if colic might in fact come from similar painful smooth muscle contractions (perhaps of the smooth muscle in the intestine) also related to low progesterone levels. Perhaps colicky infants are those whose bodies make an abnormally low amount of progesterone. High levels of progesterone from the placenta would protect these infants during the first few days of life, explaining why colic has a delayed onset after birth.

Progesterone deficiency as a cause of colic is an attractive hypothesis because progesterone, and its related chemical products, are potent central nervous system depressors. For example, in adults large doses can induce sleep or anesthesia. It would make sense that infants with low progesterone levels—and thus less central nervous system depression—might be more intense, fretful, difficult to soothe, easily startled, and have more difficulty staying asleep for long stretches.

Unfortunately, the authors of the first progesterone study also did not use an explicit definition of colic. Further, they did not "blindly" evaluate their claim that a progesteronelike drug (ethisterone) successfully treated colic. Additionally, they used a crude urinary analysis technique to determine progesterone deficiency.

To improve upon this study, we at the Children's Memorial Hospital measured plasma progesterone levels in twenty-five infants at a few weeks of age, when progesterone from their mothers would no longer be present. Infants were divided into two groups: those with colic (according to Wessel's criteria), difficult temperaments or low sensory threshold; and those without any of these features. One researcher measured plasma progesterone levels while a different researcher, working independently, made the diagnosis of colic/no colic. We found that among the infants with either colic, difficult temperament, or low sensory threshold, plasma progesterone levels were unusually low. These infants also slept for shorter periods of time and awoke more frequently at night. However, in a larger study which compared only infants with and without colic, regardless of subsequent temperament diagnosis, the group differences in levels of progesterone were less impressive, although colicky babies still had lower levels.

Colic Is Tension

A behaviorally oriented textbook had recently revived the notion that unexplained fussiness results from tension, caused either by a baby's internal "disorganization" or by external overstimulation. The paper even uses the term "stimulus-overload colic." The author argues, based only on his observations, that a child who cannot be consoled is signaling that he needs to be left alone to discharge tension by "crying it out." The author claims that letting an inconsolably fussy baby cry himself to sleep several times will end, or permanently reduce, the crying. I find this hard to believe. Three months' colic is not a behavioral problem. It cannot be prevented or cured. It is never a good idea to leave a very young infant to cry for *hours* at a time.

The not-so-hidden message here is that parental attempts to comfort a colicky baby can be counterproductive. Suddenly we are back to the idea that parents can cause or at least aggravate colic, either by overstimulating the baby physically or by passing their tension to him. Proponents of this theory like to talk about a vicious cycle of mounting tension between baby and parents. Dr. Brazelton speculated that overreacting parents can drive hypersensitive babies to greater and greater agitation, so that "what starts out as a two-hour period of crying rapidly grows to four, eight, and twelve hours." An earlier study by Dr. A. H. Stewart similarly proposes that colic occurs when unusually sensitive children are matched with unusually stimulating or unusually anxious parents.

The study conducted by Dr. Stewart in 1953 is at the source of the "tension" debate. This paper is so full of muddled reasoning and near slander against mothers and fathers of colicky babies that I am surprised to see its message still taken seriously. This shows what mischief a few unfounded conclusions can cause.

Stewart studied a small group of infant-parent pairs to see if "excessively fussy" babies received different treatment than did "quiet" babies. They did. The mothers of the fussy babies reportedly jiggled, stroked, rocked and carried their babies more; changed the babies' positions more frequently; talked to them more loudly and for longer periods. Stewart—offering no evidence beyond her own observations—implied that all this activity *caused* the fussiness, as if the babies were being pestered and jiggled to the point of breakdown. Does this follow? I don't think so. If it is possible that a lot of handling can cause the fussiness, it is equally possible that the fussiness can lead to a lot of handling. Every mother tries first one thing and then another when her baby cries. Mothers of babies who cry a great deal develop a whole repertoire of consoling motions and sounds. These responses might not appear effective to a researcher during a brief observation, but over the long run this patting and bouncing and talking could well help. Concluding that a mother's comforting gestures are the *cause* of her baby's distress appears unfounded.

Stewart made a similar error in claiming that inconsistent parenting also caused the fussiness. She reported that the mothers of the seriously fussy babies in her study alternated between holding for long stretches and not holding at all, between overfeeding and underfeeding, between overattentiveness and neglect. I doubt that any but the most distraught mothers behave as negligently and erratically as Stewart makes it appear, but I do believe that mothers of colicky infants do behave inconsistently toward their babies. This is to be expected; colic changes from day to day; what seemed to comfort the baby this morning might not work tonight. A mother who tries to remain consistent in her response to a wildly fluctuating condition will be left behind. A colicky baby needs a flexible, adaptive, improvisational kind of management. The inconsistent behavior which Stewart suspects of inflaming, if not causing, colic is more likely a reaction to it, and an appropriate one at that.

What of the theory that an infant can "pick up" tension from his parents? This is one of those oft-repeated ideas which has no basis in fact. Brazelton says that tension in the people around a crying infant makes the infant's intestinal tract act up, causing the pain, gas, drawn-up knees, etc. of colic, as though colic were some sort of infantile ulcer! Stewart says that when a tense, anxious, or ambivalent parent holds a baby, the tension is communicated through all the baby's senses (including smell!). This is folk medicine at best. At worst, it is another twist on blaming the mother's behavior, personality, or her perfectly natural anxiety.

I continue to believe that attempting to console your colicky baby through whatever means occur to you is the best approach. Something *inside* your baby is causing his distress. Your soothing motions, murmuring sounds, and close holding can only help. Of course, it is important that you do not let yourself become exhausted, depressed, or tense. The calmer you are, the more help you will be to your baby, and the better you and the rest of your family will come through this brief but trying period of colic.

Several Physiological Disturbances

Colic may be the outward expression of more than one disturbance. There are not that many ways that a one- or two-month-old bundle of organs and nerve endings can express discomfort and/or some kind of physical dishar-mony—long periods of crying is one, inability to sleep well is another. It is probably wrong to think that every baby diagnosed as "colicky" suffers the same underlying problem. I suspect that the reason one cause of colic has eluded us for so long is that there isn't just one.

There are probably several related or unrelated physiological disturbances which are capable of causing colic. In some instances, the predominant symptom might be the crying spells; in other instances the crying might be less of a problem than the symptom of inability to sleep well. The problems may not be entirely physiological; and it is also possible that different physiological disturbances in infants of no real medical significance trigger irregular, inconsistent or deliberately inattentive parenting, which in turn aggravates (not causes) excessive crying, sleep disturbances, and/or difficult temperaments.

While the causes of nighttime crying aren't clearly defined, there are ways you can help your infant—and yourself—to a good night's sleep. Suggestions many parents have found helpful are in the next chapter.

Chapter 9

Living with Colic

The bad news is that there is at present no cure for colic. The good news is that there are ways to manage colic until it goes away of its own accord when your baby is anywhere from three to five months of age.

You have already taken several important steps. You have learned all you can about colic. You have identified fallacies and old wives' tales. You have stopped blaming yourself. You understand that colic will not harm your baby and that it will come to an end. Here are some more concrete suggestions:

Soothing Your Colicky Infant

Rhythmic motions are the most effective method of soothing your infant. Use a cradle, rocking chair, or "snuggly"; take the baby for automobile rides or simply walk with him. Rocking motions may be gentle movements or vigorous swinging, depending on what your child responds to. Jiggling or bouncing may calm your baby. Some parents claim that raising and lowering the baby like an elevator ride is effective. Recently there has been talk about "baby massage" as a way to calm colicky babies. These are all really the same thing—rhythm, compression, motion. Swaddling or gently wrapping also seems to help some infants.

Be careful, however, not to bombard your baby with stimuli. Try to appeal to one sense at a time: tactile (rubbing, kissing, rocking, patting, changing from hip to shoulder, etc.), auditory (singing, humming, playing music, running the vacuum cleaner), sight (bright lights, mobiles, television). Most likely, doing too many of these things simultaneously has a stimulating rather than a relaxing effect.

Try to synchronize your actions with your baby's rhythms. If he is tense, taut, with deep exhausted heaving sobs and little physical movement, try rubbing his back ever so gently or moving your cheek over his in a slow rhythm which coincides with his breathing pattern. If he is boxing with his fists, jerking his legs and arching his back, maybe a ride on your shoulders will grab his attention and arrest the spell. You will find that after a while you become attuned to nuances within your baby's rhythms and respond accordingly.

Sucking is soothing. Sometimes a pacifier, a finger, or bottle temporarily calms the baby. Do not assume that when your baby eagerly takes a bottle he is necessarily hungry. Many colicky babies suck more liquid than they need and spit up much of what they swallowed. If you are nursing, remember that just because a bottle of formula or water calms your baby, this does not mean that there is a nursing problem.

Useless Remedies

Be skeptical about the supposed miracles accomplished with hot water bottles, herbal teas, or recordings of womb sounds. There has been a great deal of nonsense written about burping techniques, nipple sizes and nipple shapes, baby bottle straws, feeding and sleep positions, lamb's wool pads, diets for nursing mothers, special formulas, pacifiers and solid foods. These items have nothing to do with colic, crying, temperament, or sleeping habits. (You will read in Chapter 12 about the great myth of introducing solid foods to promote better sleep.)

Many useless remedies can be purchased without a prescription. One popular pellet contains chamomile, calcium phosphate, coffee, and a very small amount of active belladonna chemicals (0.0000095 percent). Another remedy contains natural blackberry flavor, Jamaica ginger, oil of anise, oil of nutmeg, and 2 percent alcohol. Maybe enough alcohol will sedate some infants! Please read labels carefully—any natural substance, flavoring agent or herb might have pharmacologic effects. Call a school of pharmacy or a medical school to find experts in pharmagnosy, the study of natural herbs and plants, to find out if a particular plant or herb is dangerous.

Also be *cautious* in using home remedies. One mother almost killed her baby by giving a mixture of Morton's Salt Substitute with lactobacillus acidophilus culture, as prescribed in the popular book, *Let's Have Healthy Children* by Adelle Davis.

Everything Works . . . for a While

When you believe that something is going to calm your baby—herbal tea, womb recordings, lamb's wool blankets, you name it—often it appears to work, for a while. You are emotionally expecting relief because you trust the advice of an authority. Your fatigue may breed inflated hopes for a cure, and the day by day variability in infant crying creates the illusion that a particular remedy works, but only for a while. What really is happening is a placebo effect, here, the emotional equivalent of an optical illusion.

Mothers may fool themselves into believing that their baby is better because of a new formula or special tea. Of course, reality sets in after a few days and shatters this illusion. Some mothers sincerely believe that their babies habituate to, or become accustomed to, the benefits from the new formula or tea much like the dope addict needs increased doses to produce the desired feeling. Some doctors believe the mothers' reports and agree that the babies really did improve for a day or two because the babies received *novel* stimulation.

Novelty is unlikely to be important because parents report that upon reintroduction, weeks after the special tea or gimmick was discarded, they see no improvement. In other words, there was no placebo effect the second time around. Naturally, if the baby coincidentally outgrows colic when a useless remedy is introduced, the mother, the family, and even the doctor might become convinced that the useless remedy actually cured the colic!

Nightlights

If your baby cries at night, darken his room. Infants are not afraid of the dark. Colic is not the expression of bad dreams. A light burning in a closet or even a conventional seven-watt nightlight can keep a sensitive baby from sleeping well. If you are absolutely convinced that your baby will not sleep in a totally black room, I would suggest using a guide light (quarter watt), which produces a faint yellow glow.

Feeding Your Colicky Baby

Keep reminding yourself that colic is not indigestion. It is not caused by formula or breast milk. Switching from one formula to the other will not help stop the crying.

If you are nursing and fear your baby is crying from hunger—nearly all nursing mothers wonder at times if they have enough milk—arrange to have the baby weighed at a doctor's office several times over the course of a week or two. Chances are you will find her gaining weight nicely.

Do not let colic make you give up breastfeeding if you want to continue. Your baby is still getting all the benefits of breast milk, even if she seems at times not to appreciate them. If you stick with it, you can look forward to many calm, pleasant months of nursing once the colic has run its course.

Still, nursing a colicky baby is undeniably a challenge. When nursing, infants with colic tend to be gulpers, twisters, forceful suckers. Sometimes they seem to reject the breast entirely. The determined nursing mother is in a bind: it is difficult to nurse a tense, twisting infant, but this is one of the few maneuvers that appears to calm the child (at least temporarily). The mother finds herself nursing very often—either because she interprets the colic as hunger cries or simply to get some peace. She is often rewarded with painful, cracked nipples and/or exhaustion. Recreational nursing may calm baby but it is no picnic for mother! Here is a description of the nursing predicament by the mother of one of my young patients:

The first three weeks of Michael's life led me to believe that having a baby would be a breeze. His behavior was almost identical from day to day. He was very calm, and so were my husband and I. Michael would eat—breastfeeding about eight to ten minutes on each side. He had no problems burping after each meal. Then I'd either hold him a while, lay him on his back, and talk or play with him. The usual schedule from the time he got up until he went to sleep would be one to one and a half hours. He would usually sleep anywhere from two and a half to four hours. Everyone would say to me, "Boy, are you ever lucky to have such a good baby."

As the fourth week approached, Michael's behavior changed drastically. He no longer wanted to sleep during the day. I felt like all he wanted was my breast. I concluded that he either was continually hungry or had strong sucking needs.

By the middle of each afternoon I was exhausted. Almost every hour I found myself breastfeeding. Sometimes I could put him off for two hours, but he'd cry a lot. I'd change his diaper, walk him, hold him, rock him, sing to him, change his position and so on. Nothing would please him except my breast, which was terribly tiring, to say the least. The thing that saved our lives is that he slept long hours through the night—probably because he was exhausted from being up all day. The worst times were midafternoon, and again between 5:00 P.M. and 10:00 P.M., after which he would sleep for around five hours straight. He would fuss and cry, and nothing would calm him except when he was nursing.

If you are in a predicament similar to this mother's give yourself some relief by trying the following suggestions:

1. Space feedings a few hours apart. One mother said, "I must have 'Chinese' breast milk; he gets hungry just one hour after nursing." If you last nursed your baby well less than two hours

ago (not a snack or a sip), he has no room in his stomach for more milk and your breasts contain no milk for him. Nursing too frequently is pointless, and if it causes you pain or exhaustion, it is destructive. See if your baby will accept a pacifier instead. Try different kinds, maybe you will find one he likes.

2. Ask your doctor about hydrocortisone ointment. A famous pediatric dermatologist at the Children's Memorial Hospital who nursed her own children suggests treating cracked nipples with 1 percent hydrocortisone ointment. It is safe for mother and baby, and seems to work better than any other treatment. Many of my patients' mothers have reported rapid healing of sore nipples by using this treatment.

3. Don't exhaust yourself. One mother of a colicky infant stored breast milk so that her husband could feed the baby once during the night and her mother could handle a similar daytime feeding. In this way she was able to get some extra rest. When the baby was several weeks old, the baby's grandmother went home and the father returned to work. Now, all alone and very busy, the mother saw her previously ample supply of breast milk dwindle to almost nothing. We discussed how she had decreased her fluid intake, how she was worried about her mother's departure and generally under strain. I reassured her that while it was important to continue having the child suck at her breasts to stimulate milk production, a single bottle of formula for one or two days would not harm the baby or inhibit lactation. She increased her fluid intake, rested more, and after four to five days was again nursing with more than ample milk production. Throughout this period the child continued to have severe colic spells with periods of inconsolable crying. This mother knew that the crying was not related to nursing.

Another mother of one of my patients felt especially bad when nursing failed to calm her baby:

It's early evening and my daughter is screaming and restless. Nothing seems to calm her, not even nursing. I didn't think Chelsea was colicky but she sure was fussy. Although her fussiness was not an everyday occurrence, it persisted from her second or third week of life until about two months of age.

At first I thought something I was eating was causing her to have gas. Then I felt her behavior was due to my inexperience as a mother. As these episodes continued, I began to feel inadequate, desperate, sad and exhausted.

I felt inadequate as a parent. I didn't know what to do to comfort my child, or whether what I was doing was right. *I especially felt inadequate when Chelsea rejected my breast.* It seemed as if nothing could console and comfort her.

We had visions of a child who would be comforted at the touch of her mom or dad. Soon all the sleepless nights and exaggerated feelings of incompetency led to exhaustion. Would this cycle ever end? Well, it finally did. With the help of our pediatrician, we soon began to realize that this behavior was normal and would not last indefinitely. I also found that her fussiness was neither caused nor enhanced by my behavior. Along with this realization came the light at the end of the tunnel. I then knew her fussiness would not last forever.

I became aware of certain behavioral changes that manifested themselves either before or after each fussy period. She would startle easily, have difficulty falling asleep and then would sleep for shorter periods of time. Also, during her fussy periods she exhibited different behavioral characteristics. She was restless and would scream with a quivering chin. She would become stiff or have rigid movements. She would not nurse, or when she did she would suck frantically. She would become overtired but would not sleep. Sometimes she would be wide awake one moment and sound asleep a second later.

Chelsea is now three months old. Her fussy periods have ceased and she wakes in the morning with a smile that lasts all day. We really love our "perfect" child.

Sometimes a nursing mother notices that the baby seems calmer in her husband's arms than in her own. She may feel that her husband does a better job of soothing the baby, that perhaps the baby "prefers" him to her. What is really happening is quite simple. The baby recognizes that his mother is the source of milk. When she holds him he quite naturally squirms and twists, rooting around, looking to suck, even when he is not hungry.

Physicians should encourage the mother's desire to nurse her colicky baby. It is an important accomplishment for both of them. One mother called me when her colicky baby was exactly three months old. She was determined to continue nursing and to start working part-time. Her husband was a fireman and found it very difficult to be around his crying baby on days off. She was under enormous stress. All her friends claimed that if she would feed her baby formula, then the crying would disappear. She wanted to—and did—keep on nursing after the colic disappeared to show them, and herself, that nursing was not the cause of the crying. Here is a report from the mother of another one of my patients; persevering with nursing helped her maintain her confidence and self-esteem:

> Both my husband and I questioned our best judgments and our ability to care for Lisa. At one point I questioned my ability to nurse and felt that I was literally poisoning my baby. Her screaming episodes came a predictable ten minutes after every feeding. At times I felt tortured. I consider myself a rational and caring person, yet often found myself crying in the shower or praying that my husband could somehow relieve the tension, anger, and helplessness that I felt.
>
> At six weeks, Lisa seemed to be easing into patterns and appeared finally to be getting good, deep sleep. Her smiling times were numerous, but she still had hours of monstrous screaming. I overcame my fear of nursing and decided to continue weeks after I had planned to stop. Nursing became the one pleasurable experience the baby and I had together. When I finally did wean Lisa it was a sad time; we were separate after being together for so long.

Your Relationship with Your Colicky Baby

Colic strikes during the early months when the parent-child relationship is just forming. Daily bouts of screaming, with the attendant guilt and worry, can, of course, interfere with this relationship. You must keep reminding yourself that although your baby is in distress, he is *not* rejecting you or commenting on your ability as a parent.

Parents should be especially aware of their behavior toward their baby during the first few months, particularly when the baby is calm and alert and social interaction is possible. These times will become more frequent as your baby approaches his three-month birthday, and should be taken advantage of. Although your behavior won't have an effect on the run of colic, it will have an accumulative effect in the sense that you're learning a way of responding to your child. If you tend to respond in a tense, anxious manner, even when your baby isn't crying, this not only robs you of enjoying those "good" times, but can influence your baby's behavior when the bout with colic is over. When your baby is fussy, drowsy, or both, he is almost out of reach. If your baby cries when awake and/or doesn't rest well when asleep, he is probably not going to be very sociable, attentive, or receptive to the messages you send him. It is crucial that you shower your baby with attention during those times when he is awake and not crying, and prepare for a burst of interaction as soon as the colic goes away.

Do not let the colic throw you off balance. Love your crybaby all the time. If you are able to respond calmly, you will be able to enjoy your baby more during the nonfussy periods and your baby will enjoy you more. When a baby's colicky behavior adversely affects the mother's behavior, they can reinforce each other's distress. Remember to treat your infant in the same loving way whether he is crying or content. How the child's temperament and sleeping patterns will ultimately turn out are probably related more to your behavior during this time than to the original physiologic disturbance(s) that caused the colic.

Take Care of Yourself

A colicky baby needs a great deal of attention. You may find your life filled with rocking, walking, feeding, and soothing. But the truth is, most of what you will be doing about the colic is waiting it out. Try to keep up *your* health, good cheer, and loving relationships during this difficult time. Don't forget about yourself, and the rest of your family. Then you will all be ready to give the baby your best love and care.

It is normal for parents to be angry, bewildered, frustrated and guilty about feeling that way. Resolve to break that circle right now. You have had an unlucky break and you are entitled to feel resentful sometimes. Maintaining a sense of humor is hard, but any mother with a colicky infant will feel better getting her feelings out into the open.

Whenever possible, the mother should have her husband, friends, or babysitter take over care of the screamer so that she can get away. If you feel reluctant, remember that your baby's crying will not be as bothersome to a "stranger" as it is to you, his mother. This is not self-indulgence—you *must* have frequent breaks from your colicky baby.

As we have seen from studies on crying, responding promptly and consistently when a baby under three months cries is better than waiting to see if he settles down. He probably won't, and the time you spend waiting and listening is unpleasant for you. On the other hand, if none of your efforts seem to calm the baby, it is not necessary to exhaust yourself. If you run out of energy and find he is as unhappy in your arms as in his crib, put him down and let him cry. A baby in the midst of a truly inconsolable spell of colic probably does not know whether he is being held or not. A popular recommendation is to try for fifteen or twenty minutes to soothe the child; if you see no results, put him down for about half an hour and then try again. In my experience, most mothers are able to, and want to, spend more than twenty minutes soothing their babies but are not willing to endure even half an hour of crying. Spend as much time as you can with your baby, but do not feel compelled to spend six or eight solid hours consoling him without a break. Many fathers have experienced the pleasure of automobile rides at three in the morning with their baby to give their wives a break. Fathers quickly learn how hard it is to be a loving parent and husband while always on the verge of falling asleep.

Creative Parenting

I believe that over the long run, creative parental behavior will override whatever transient physiological disturbances are causing colic. The problem is that some parents—especially mothers—become so distraught or fatigued that it prevents calm, thought-out parenting. Conflict can erupt among family members over how to handle the problem. Husband and wife may expend energy blaming each other. Everyone's self-esteem can suffer, and no one will have the resourcefulness to try strategies which might end up helping. So try to get enough rest, keep your wits about you, and get away for occasional quiet evenings.

Treating Colic with Medicine

There is a case for treating colic with medication. When the crying becomes so disruptive that neither the child nor the parents are getting any sleep, intervention should be tried. Some mothers are physically unable to spend hours trying to comfort colicky babies; they may be tired from the delivery or have other children to attend to. The father may have to get his sleep in order to work. They may find themselves truly unable to cope because of exhaustion. When colic leads to sleep deprivation in the baby or severely disrupts family life, it's time to consider medication.

A commonly used drug for treating colic is dicyclomine. It is not a narcotic, analgesic, anesthetic, hypnotic, barbiturate, tranquilizer, or sedative. Dicyclomine is a smooth muscle relaxant believed to reduce colicky behavior by easing spasms of the muscle lining the intestines. However, it is possible that the drug works instead on the central nervous system, calming the infant in general.

Parents often describe their infants' reaction to the drug this way: "the colic melts away," or "my out-of-control baby became calm and nursed easily within 60 minutes of taking the medicine." I have videotaped this remarkably rapid behavioral change. Even when dicyclomine does not make the colic go away entirely, parents report that it makes the spells shorter or less frequent, or makes the child more consolable. While some infants do become drowsy with excessive dosages, most often they become alert and calm rather than "drugged."

Dicyclomine is the only drug approved by the Food and Drug Administration as probably effective for the treatment of colic. All other drugs suggested for the treatment of colic either have not been studied properly or have been found to be no better than a placebo. Dicyclomine has proved decisively superior to the placebo in several studies. The onset of action is very rapid; you will know within several hours whether it helps or not and you do not have to treat your baby for days to find out if this medicine is going to be effective.

In 1959, Illingworth studied twenty infants with colic (defined as inconsolable evening screaming spells in healthy infants). Dicyclomine or a placebo was randomly dispensed by a pharmacist participating in the study. While Illingworth concluded that dicyclomine produced improvement, he performed no statistical analysis of the data. Therefore, there remained a possibility that the apparent drug benefit occurred by chance alone.

In 1977, a similar double-blind study was performed on twenty-five babies using a definition of colic similar to Illingworth's. Dicyclomine again was found to be superior to a placebo. The statistical analysis performed showed that this improvement was unlikely to have been a chance occurrence. Recent studies at the Children's Memorial Hospital have also shown dicyclomine to be an effective treatment for colic.

Dicyclomine is sold as Bentyl and is available only by prescription. Side effects from this drug which occur when the dose is too high include excessive drowsiness and a decrease in the number of times the baby urinates. Both of these side effects may last several hours after the drug is discontinued. But many mothers are, understandably, reluctant to give prescriptive drugs to their infants unless it's absolutely necessary. If your baby is crying seemingly without end and you are considering asking your pediatrician about prescribing this medication, perhaps the following account by a mother who gave her baby Bentyl to control colic will help you in the decision. This account will also illustrate the points we have covered prior to the discussion of medication.

May 9, 1983

"Mrs. Lazar, you have the calmest baby we've ever seen! He slept so soundly we had to wake him for his 2:00 A.M. feeding. He's perfect—congratulations!"

If this is all true, how come he won't stop crying? Someone must have switched babies on me in the hospital because this can't be the same one. This baby is having a horrible time—he literally cried for ten hours straight. Nothing works. Not rocking. Not feeding. All babies cry, I reason. But deep down I know it's not like this. A small wave of panic grips me—what if something is really wrong? We call Dr. Weissbluth and describe the symptoms; he reassures us that the baby is okay and asks us to stay in touch with him. I have this strange feeling I'd better buckle my seatbelt—we're heading for a stormy time.

May 10, 1983

The crying continues. On, and on, and on. This time it's eighteen hours. I'm convinced Christopher must be starving. Nothing comforts him for very long—only lots of nursing. We must have talked with the doctor a hundred times already. We're desperate. Finally, the doctor suggests that John take Christopher for a car ride so I can rest. Poor John rides around for two hours. In the meantime I'm so wired I can't sleep.

May 11, 1983

Our doctor agrees to see us at his home. We're so grateful—especially when he tells us that Christopher is very healthy. I blurt out my very unscientific findings about colic based on a popular child-care book I've read but surprisingly the doctor doesn't laugh. He explains to us that Christopher is too young to be diagnosed as having colic so for right now we'll call it "unexplained crying." That's okay with me. So long as he tells me Christopher is fine he can call it anything he wants. It's hard to believe Christopher is already one week old. Actually, I'm very surprised I remember that at all. Our days just sort of blend into our nights. About the only way I can tell the difference is that I change into a different bathrobe for my "midnight shift."

May 12, 1983

I'm thirty-two today, but I feel like a bigger baby than my son. Normally, I am a pretty confident lady but all of this crying has reduced me to a wimp. Humor has always carried me through the worst of times but I am having a terrible time finding it right now. My heart just breaks when Christopher starts screaming. It's crying like I've never heard—full of pain and anger. His legs bunch up and his little fists just thrash around. One minute he seems okay, the next he's crying harder and harder until I think he'll burst. We take turns walking with him, rocking him, soothing him—nothing works. Finally out of sheer exhaustion (I'm sure) Christopher goes to sleep. It's so hard to believe this beautiful sleeping baby has any care in the world. I've got to get stronger for him. But first I've got to sleep!

May 13, 1983

Oh, the advice that's pouring in!

"Obviously, it's your milk. . . . Put a hot water bottle next to him. . . . He's starving . . . Are you *sure* that there's nothing wrong with him. . . . My cousin had a baby. . . . Molasses is the answer." And on and on. The doctor warned me about all of the advice I'd be getting. I thought I could ignore it but I am getting so delirious even my crazy Aunt Martha's advice is starting to make sense to me. But the little reasoning powers I have left must prevail. Christopher has gained weight and the doctor must know what he's doing. Now repeat after me, Marlena, one hundred times—everything's going to be okay.

May 14, 1983

On the advice of Christopher's doctor, I leave the house for the first time today. I'm beginning to relate real well to run-away Moms—women who say they are going to return from the store in an hour and show up twenty years later. Seriously, although I didn't exactly believe the doctor when he said it would give me a new lease on life, it really was a much needed break—I was delighted to see him again even though he was sobbing, and I think he was happy to see me too. So what if I called six times in two hours. I promise to get better.

May 15, 1983

My first Mother's Day and what a day it's been! Eighteen straight hours of crying. About the only break in the action was when John took Christopher for a long car ride. Ironically, Christopher slept the entire time. The minute John returned with him he started up again. I am almost embarrassed to say we just broke up laughing. We finally got to sleep about 4:00 A.M.—John on the couch and me on the spare bed with Christopher. I held him very close to me, stroking his hair and whispering to him, praying he'd sleep just a little. He looks so tired! So does Daddy, Mommy and Grandma. Finally it happens. It's only for two hours but I feel rejuvenated and full of hope that this nightmare will end.

May 16, 1983

I am so involved with Christopher I almost forgot that today I'm supposed to interview a lady that will be his caretaker when I return to work in July. July? I must be kidding! I can't even tell you what day it is. I make a valiant attempt at putting myself together. My, how things have changed! I used to get the shakes if I didn't have mascara on. Now I'm lucky if I can manage to comb my hair. Anyway, right before this lady shows up I make a deal with Christopher. I promise to drive him around in the car all night if he won't cry while she's here. Sure enough he cooperates! I mean not *one* tear!

She raves on and on about what a wonderful baby he is. Finally, I break down and confess that he spends a large part of his day crying. I expect the woman to bolt for the door but instead she tells me she has experienced this with not one but *two* babies. So what's another one! I have to pinch myself! Needless to say, she has the job.

May 19, 1983

Misery sure loves company. I talked with a woman today who is going through the same thing as we are. It's nice not being the "Lone Ranger" but my heart really went out to her. She's been up for almost two days rocking, nursing, and walking. Her baby is about one month older than Christopher and it's been like that almost from the beginning. How well I understand her frustration and helplessness! And lest we forget, the terrible exhaustion.

May 21, 1983

It's such a beautiful day that I decided to throw fate to the wind and go on an outing with Baby Lazar. I can't believe it—he sleeps the entire time we're out. "Every baby should be as good," someone says. "What a great baby." This has got to be "The Twilight Zone."

May 22, 1983

The morning is dreadful but we manage to make it through another day. Actually, John and I are getting pretty good at dealing with all of the crying. What a team we make—kind of the Starsky and Hutch of the colic set. When one reaches the deep end, the other takes over. We have had our tense moments but this experience has made us and our marriage so much stronger. Besides, divorce is totally out of the question—neither of us can handle sole custody! (Only kidding.)

May 23, 1983

We're beginning to have more contact with the outside world and I am glad for that (I started worrying myself when I went to the grocery store and began babbling with the cashier). I'm getting more daring, too. Christopher and I went shopping for the first time—only lasted for about an hour, but at least we tried, and we're going to try more and more each day. I refuse to let this beat us!

May 24, 1983

The doctor asked me to look for a pattern to the crying but there isn't any. Sometimes it's morning, sometimes it's afternoon, less so at night. He's simply never the same. About the only predictable thing is that it will happen for one hour at a time or for six or ten hours. Maybe that's why it's easier to deal with—the certainty of it. No, that's a lie. It's never easy.

May 25, 1983

The beat goes on. Christopher isn't sleeping very much and seems to want to nurse almost every hour on the hour. I held him for almost sixteen hours today on the sofa like a zombie. The rest of the day was spent walking and walking some more. Poor John is interviewing for a new job and has to sit on the edge of the chair during his appointment so he doesn't fall asleep. Give us a break, Christopher!

May 26, 1983

More crying. More nursing. More of the same. Car rides, stroller rides, loud music, rocking, and walking aren't working at all today. When Christopher finally sleeps I am sure it's crib death. I'm at his side most of the time just watching him. I am too tired to sleep, too wired to relax. Oh, my baby, when is this going to get better?

May 27, 1983

Ta da! Help is on the way! This morning we took Christopher to see the doctor for his check-up. With so many phone calls each day, we are well acquainted by now. Christopher spends a great deal of the time there crying. Neither the doctor's soothing voice nor my nursing can calm him—he's in real misery. Very carefully (as though he could read my mind) the doctor tells us we may be able to make life easier for all of us—some medication for Christopher. My first reaction is one of quiet horror. God, he's not even one month old and we're going to drug him up. John is far more receptive to the suggestion. Maybe because he's a chemist and a lot more logical than I am right now. Frankly, I'm torn. I want so desperately to help Christopher but I'm having a hard time with the idea of giving him medicine. As the doctor explains what it may do or may not do, I start to get a grip on myself. It's as simple as this: we can go on as we are or we can hope to improve it. Suddenly, there isn't a choice—we've got to go for it.

May 28, 1983

The name of the medicine is dicylomine. We have to call three drugstores before we can find one that can fill it. I'm very brave about it until it comes time to actually giving it to him, then I panic. I can't bear to watch John give it to him, let alone give it myself. (Mind you this is the same woman who could give injections to her grandmother when she was terminally ill.) I have to walk out of the room because I'm crying so hard.

May 29, 1983

It seems the medication either works or doesn't. What I mean by that is that you see an improvement right away or it's not the solution. Luckily, we see an immediate improvement. Christopher's still crying, but a lot less. For the first time in weeks he actually takes a nap in the afternoon and so do I. We're still sleeping together on the spare bed and I wake up holding him very close to me. He sleeps so soundly and peacefully. Please, God, let this last just a little longer.

May 30, 1983

This seems too good to be true. I am pinching myself a lot. Yes, there's still crying—mostly in the morning and late afternoon—but it's far more manageable. So far, Christopher hasn't experienced any side effects from the medication—no drowsiness or inability to nurse. I am starting to feel better about giving it to him. I guess only time will tell.

May 31, 1983

A very tough morning, but otherwise a pretty good day. The crying was very intense before his morning shot of medicine but Christopher seemed to improve dramatically as the day continued. How can I argue with something that obviously seems to work? Christopher still has his bad moments, but at least now he has some goods ones too. I have to keep a positive attitude about this. We *are* helping him!

June 1, 1983

Wow! I am starting to feel like the *National Enquirer* with all of these colic confessions I'm hearing. The producer I've worked with for three years finally confessed that his baby didn't have a virus all those times he was up all night—it was colic. My husband had it, too. And so did his aunt and uncle, the lady next door's baby, my second cousin, more than I can mention. Maybe I'm onto some sort of fad here. I can joke about colic today because I've had five straight hours of sleep. What bliss!

June 2, 1983

Things aren't going well. Christopher cries from 5:00 A.M. to 10:00 A.M. without missing a beat. Then he suddenly stops. We get a reprieve until about 4:00 P.M. when he wakes from a nap that lasts only fifteen minutes. The decision is made to increase the amount of medicine from three doses to four, the additional one to be given at around 10:00 P.M. My whole day seems to revolve around crying, nursing, and the medication. I feel very cheated. I imagine every new mother in America taking long walks with their babies, cooing by the hours with them, waiting eagerly for them to awake from their long nap. Not me. I'm covered in dicyclomine stains, practically comatose. Boy, will I appreciate the time when Christopher gets over this.

June 3, 1983

The extra dosage of the medication helps through the morning and part of the afternoon, too. I am so encouraged that we take advantage of a sunny day and go to the park. I am so tired that I am afraid that I might fall sleep on the park bench and be arrested for vagrancy. But it's so nice just to get out!

June 4, 1983

Christopher is one month old. We've had a terrible night. I fed him four times during the night, then at 5:00 A.M. But after the nursing he kept crying off and on. John walked him for a while, then I did. He finally fell back to sleep after his medicine, but I was so frustrated I stayed wide awake. My entire being aches—especially my heart. Christopher is such a lovely baby when he's not in pain. He's probably as frustrated about this as I am.

June 12, 1983

It's our seventh wedding anniversary. We spend a "romantic evening" collapsed on the sofa. I think we're starting to adjust our life to colic. We're able to sleep at the drop of a hat, eat our dinner in ten seconds flat, and oh, what rhythm we have on those midnight strolls. Best of all, we're developing a sense of humor about it. When we stop and think about all of the things that could have happened to Christopher, we should be very grateful that it's only colic.

June 14, 1983

Important colic discovery made today: one-half teaspoon dicyclomine plus one very boring Cubs game equals one delightful nap for Mom and baby. I wonder what the good doctor will say about this theory?

June 15, 1983

Christopher continues his "nursing marathon," but I'm managing. What I'm having a tough time managing is all of the unsolicited advice I'm getting again. On some days we don't know which end is up, but when you try to evaluate it, you think that having a baby shouldn't be this difficult, this perplexing. Right along with all of your doubts, fears, and fatigue come the advice and admonitions from everyone. Enough is enough!

June 16, 1983

My girlfriend frantically calls me today. She recently had a baby and he, too, is showing definite colic signs—constant crying, constant nursing, constant misery. I do everything in my power not to give her any advice but I can't help myself—I know how utterly frustrated and helpless she feels. Besides telling her the obvious things to try I shock myself by mentioning dicyclomine. It's probably the first time I've said it out loud. Before I know it, I'm expounding on its virtues like a 30-second commercial. My, how things have changed.

June 20 to June 30, 1983

On the whole, it's been a pretty "even" time for us. The crying bouts are much better—in fact, almost predictable. I know, for instance, that there will be one either in the morning or late afternoon. Sometimes they last as long as an hour or as little as ten minutes. A lot of people are horrified when I mention this, but we're very encouraged. After all, it's not ten hours anymore and we know he eventually stops. I guess it's safe to say we've seen the worst and there's no place to go but up.

July 2, 1983

There is no justice, no logic, to what we're experiencing right now. The sooner you realize this the better off you are. You learn to grab time whenever you can because you never know when your time is going to be grabbed back from you. But little by little you learn how to manage your life again. It takes time. It takes patience. It takes a lot of hard work. But you're a better, stronger person for it.

July 3, 1983

The doctor gave me a real boost today by telling me I can look forward to more "breakthrough behavior" in Christopher. Translated, that means even less crying—I guess. We're already enjoying him more and I can't wait for this to happen.

July 4, 1983

Christopher is two months old today. How the weeks go by! John and I are still sleep-deprived and still a little bit overwhelmed with the demands of the baby, and there are times when it seems life will always be like this. But there are some wonderful moments, too, and more of them all the time. Christopher is becoming more responsive to us; today for the first time even he smiled. I wasn't quite sure that's what is was, but the next time I *knew*, and it was fabulous. When you think about it, it's hard to remember what life was like before we had him. Just one terrific moment with Christopher erases all the bad ones.

July 7 to July 11, 1983

Someone switched babies on me again. We journeyed to Detroit to christen Christopher. I almost had the shakes over the prospect of traveling with him in the car for over five hours, but he just sailed through it. He slept the *entire* way. And that was true for the entire time we were there, too. An earthquake couldn't wake him at night. Of course, our colic story is looking very suspect. It's even looking suspect to us.!

July 12, 1983

Christopher's caretaker started today. I wanted to be home with her before I returned to work to make sure she learned our routine. Routine! Who am I kidding? Every day is totally different from the last. I'm a little anxious to see how she'll deal with the colic. It's one thing to say it won't bother you and quite another to experience it first hand. Although there *is* a marked improvement in it, it still happens.

July 13, 1983

The doctor and his nurse convince me that it's time to wean Mommy from Christopher. Now that we have some help, I'm encouraged to go for long lunches, visit friends, etc. The goal is to get me to relax so I can continue nursing—something I really want to do. Well, I follow doctor's orders and last a total of one hour before I call. And during my phone call I notice something very weird—I'm rocking and swaying as though I'm carrying Christopher! Talk about separation anxiety!

July 14, 1983

The amount of dicyclomine is increased, because again Christopher has grown considerably since May. He is not experiencing such violent attacks these days, but I don't really know how he is. Is his colic better or is it the medication? I allow myself for a moment to think that we might be at the end of it . . .

July 19, 1983

For the first time in a really long time, we have an "official" bad day. Christopher cries for most of the morning, afternoon, and part of the night. At about 8:00 P.M. we really panic when he vomits, and we call the doctor—again. But by the time we're off the phone Christopher is sleeping soundly.

July 21, 1983

We accidentally skip our afternoon dose of medication and really pay for it later. Christopher is in misery for four hours even after we give him his medicine. Sometimes I worry that we'll have to do this forever.

July 22, 1983

My last full day home for a while. I'm a little sad, a little anxious about starting work tomorrow. The time has just flown by! I have to confess it wasn't exactly how I envisioned it when I was pregnant. In between my baby's long naps I would write all those great articles, make those wonderful gourmet meals for John, and read all those books I'd been meaning to read. It didn't exactly work out that way. The only writing I managed to do was in this diary, my favorite meals were from carry-out and I was lucky to get to page two in the newspaper. On the bright side, I've grown to know Christopher far better than I'd ever dreamed. I think, too, I've learned to be a Mom a lot quicker than many. Yes, there was a lot of crying, hair pulling, and exhaustion, but I wouldn't change a thing. Well, maybe a couple . . .

July 24, 1983

Juggling work and a new baby is a real challenge, to say the least. But when I arrive at home these days I'm finding a happy Christopher. He seems so relieved that he's not having so many colic attacks. So are we. Our fingers are crossed that this will continue.

July 25 to July 31, 1983

It's been pretty boring at the Lazars' lately. Thank heaven! We're down to one dose of dicyclomine three times a day. Christopher isn't too thrilled when he has to take it now but once it's over, he's a content baby. He smiles and readily babbles—a genuine pleasure to be around.

August 1, 1983

Just when you thought it was safe to say things are better, up pops a new thing. Christopher, not one of the world's all-time great sleepers, now has decided that the hours between 1:00 A.M. and 3:00 A.M. are perfect for carrying on conversations. I'm very grateful it's not crying. In fact, this babbling would be charming at 8:00 P.M. But please not all night!

August 2, 1983

The doctor thinks this latest development has something to do with my return to work. Christopher, he feels, has figured out that I'm not at home to shower attention on him in the day and now he needs some extra attention. John and I take turns soothing him when he awakes—holding his hand, stroking his hair, etc.

August 3, 1983

I can hardly believe it, but the first time we try this "comfort" routine it works—for about two hours. Although there are no tears involved, Christopher still needs a lot of nursing during the night to comfort him.

August 4, 1983

Christopher is three months old today. I'm very encouraged that the crying has greatly diminished, but I'm not convinced or confident that the colic is over. His caretaker continues to have some pretty tough moments during the day. But God bless her, she walks him, soothes him, and is marvelous at giving him his medication. What more could we ask for?

August 5, 1983

It's just as I suspected—colic can and does last longer than three months. Although the doctor says we can look forward to an even greater decrease in crying, I have horrible visions of my son going away to college and me reminding him to take his dicyclomine.

August 6, 1983

Such a glorious day! Christopher is alert, happy, and a real joy to be around. For the first time, he almost sleeps through the night. John and I are so conditioned, we stay up half the night.

August 8, 1983

He's like a different baby again today. We try to keep him on his bottle schedule but he refuses all of them. Being the tough cookie I am, I cave in immediately and spend most of the day nursing, which wears me out. Work is starting to look like a vacation.

August 8, 1983

On my one allotted phone call home, I learn that Christopher has been having an awful day. The caretaker says it reminds her of his early days when his colic was at its all-time high. I am not disappointed when I return home. I prayed a lot on the way, but he's in a lot of misery and I know we're in for some interesting times.

August 9, 1983

Luckily, the medication comes to the rescue. We give him an extra dose and he seems immediately better. Wide awake, but immediately better. We spend the night watching the news. Nothing like a well-informed baby.

August 10, 1983

A much better day for all of us. Christopher cruises through the day and the night isn't too bad, either. He's not a champion sleeper, but I'd rather have him waking up happy and ready to chat than miserable and ready to cry.

August 13, 1983

The Lazars visit the doctor. Christopher gets a clean bill of health and his shots, too. He's in a wonderful mood until late afternoon when he gets a little ill from the shots. The crying is very intense for a long time; it's like an old nightmare. We finally comfort him well enough for him to fall asleep. The irony of the whole thing is that we discussed with the doctor the possibility of weaning Christopher from the dicyclomine sometime next week. After today, I can hardly wait for that one.

August 14, 1983

Everything's okay again. Christopher is all smiles and so are we. We're "gearing up" to try life without the medication. The doctor and I agree it should be done on a day that I'm not around. I pick next Wednesday because I will have the day off. I can arrange to be out of the house, yet available in case disaster strikes. We're hoping for the best.

August 15, 1983

The caretaker is game for our experiment. I think there are two reasons why: she's as curious as we are to see if Christopher's colic is finally over and it's become harder and harder to give him the medication. Never a big fan of his medication, he's taken to spitting it out and crying furiously each time. Never a dull moment with Christopher.

August 16, 1983

He's a marvelous baby today—napping, taking his bottle, and not one tear. It's almost too good to be true! I'm a bit more confident about taking him off the medicine but I keep fluctuating. Sometimes I think I'm crazy to ruin a good thing. In one of those moments where I'm wild for adventure, I skip the late evening dosage. Oh, you mad impetuous girl!

August 17, 1983

Christopher awakens a few times during the night but otherwise he's fine. In the morning I leave as planned, determined not to telephone every five minutes. I do pretty well until early afternoon when I call home. My heart sinks as the caretaker tells me that Christopher's in a lot of pain and I ought to come home. I know how serious this must be because in all of the time she has been with us she has never sounded like this. I raced home and gave him some medicine. In a matter of minutes, he's better. It's not over yet.

August 18, 1983

We're down, but not out! It didn't work this time but we all made a pact to try it again in a few weeks. Right now, he just needs a little more help.

August 20, 1983

We're pretty much back on the dicyclomine, although I must confess that if he's sleeping (rare, I admit) during the time he's scheduled to take it, I'll skip it for a while. A schedule is something we still don't have. He is still eating around eight times a day and sleeping whenever I'm not panicked about this. He'll have the rest of his life to be on a schedule.

September 1, 1983

I am delighted to write that Christopher has had not one bout with colic in eleven days. We're very tempted to try it again without the medication but we're a bit gun shy after the last try. Maybe in a few days we can get up the courage.

September 2, 1983

Ooops! Just when you thought it was safe to go back into the water! A really awful night; the day so-so. Not nearly as bad as it used to be, but not pleasant either. Even Christopher looks frustrated!

September 3, 1983

Only one shot of dicyclomine today. Our family is visiting us and he's having the time of his life with all of these new faces. There isn't any time to have colic!

September 4, 1983

Four months old! We celebrate with a wonderful day. To look at Christopher now no one would ever guess this baby ever had a care in the world.

September 5 to September 10, 1983

We're not sleeping through the night or anything rash like that, but it's getting far more manageable—he's only up three times a night, some nights only once. John and I have his awake time down to a science—diaper change, nursing, comforting in a matter of minutes. We'd like to eliminate some of this but we're afraid to press our luck. We've come a long way since May.

September 11, 1983

We went cold turkey on the medicine and nothing happened. I think, I hope, our colic is over.

September 12, 1983

I feel it's over

September 13, 1983

I know it's over.

September 14, 1983

It's over!

Hospitalization

In the past, severely colicky babies were sometimes hospitalized. Frankly, this was done because some doctors believed that colic results from a family situation that more or less drove the baby crazy. Today, of course, we know that this is not true. Still, a doctor will occasionally propose to remove a baby from the family for a while, for "tests and observation." You should know that as long as the baby is gaining weight and exhibits no abnormalities apart from the colic symptoms discussed in this book, hospitalization will not accomplish anything. The real motive is to give the parents some relief.

If a doctor should suggest hospitalizing your severely colicky infant, talk with him very frankly. Does he have reason to believe the problem is something more than colic? Exactly what tests will be performed and what can he learn from them? Why does he feel your baby should be separated from you? What can be learned from "observing" the baby in the hospital rather than at home? You should probably get a second opinion before even considering this drastic a move.

I believe that hospitalization for colic is never justified. It is very expensive (many insurance companies balk at paying colic-related expenses), and infants can easily catch serious infections in hospitals. Having a baby in the hospital is extremely stressful on parents and it can be upsetting to the baby. Even if your baby's colic is so bad that the idea of respite looks good to you, there are many cheaper, safer alternatives: hire a full-time sitter, or even a private-duty nurse; go to a hotel for a weekend; alternate with your husband spending nights away from home; leave the baby with relatives for a day or two.

Remember that many, many parents have lived through colic. It is a trying experience, but does not really last all that long. Your colicky baby—even if her crying is very persistent and very severe—is not sick and does not belong in a hospital. She belongs at home with people who love her.

Managing Colic

Prevention of colic will be possible when the cause or causes are known. Right now, only "containment" or management measures can be taken. Based on my experience, these should start with prevention of unnecessary guilt, worry, and confusion on the part of the parents. The better they understand the nature of colic, the better off they will be. I believe that the management of colic should start at the prenatal visit with the pediatrician. Parents should be alerted before the birth of their child that colic might occur and that steps can be taken if it does. I would recommend that parents ask about colic even if the pediatrician does not bring up the subject. This is not borrowing trouble; it is being prepared.

All of the tips for living with colic given in this chapter have helped large numbers of people. The colicky months can be made bearable. Future behavioral and sleeping problems can be minimized. Nothing is more important to parents than a good dose of optimism; and colic *does* disappear. Parents will sleep again, as you'll learn through the experiences of several mothers of colicky infants, some successful and some less successful, in later chapters.

Chapter 10

As Colic Ends

Through draggy afternoons, arsenic eve-
nings, and long nights you have sometimes thought colic would
go on forever. But, eventually, when the baby is around three or
four months old, you should begin to notice a let-up in the crying.
The baby may skip days of crying, may have fewer spells, or
briefer ones. The change in her behavior may be abrupt and
dramatic, or it may be gradual and erratic. After months of disap-
pointment with temporary "improvement" cruelly followed by
even worse relapse, you may not dare believe what is happening.
But one day you will say to your husband, or he to you, "You
know, she really is a lot better."

This is certainly a time for celebration. You have lived through
colic, but you may not have reached the Promised Land yet.
Sometimes a miracle does occur, and within days the baby
becomes quiet, cheerful, relaxed, and a good sleeper. Other
children, however, do indeed cry less but remain irritable and
hard to soothe, and awaken easily from sleep. (These children
could be developing the kind of sleep problem which will be

discussed in Chapter 12.) With careful handling, you may be able to prevent these sleep problems before they get serious.

Time For a Change

During the colicky period, your child has learned to associate falling asleep with extended rocking, walking, hugging, feeding. She comes to expect this attention. She may never have learned to fall asleep by herself. She may be, in a sense, addicted to social interaction in order to fall asleep. So even after the physiological causes of the crying (whatever they are) have abated, the old fussy pattern might remain.

Parents, too, become conditioned after several months of coping with colic. They have grown used to lavishing prompt, continual attention on their crying baby. The variable nature of colic has taught them to shift strategies frequently. They have become improvisers—trying what worked last night, trying what worked this morning, or trying something new. It has never been practical for them to have a plan; they just responded. However, a post-colicky baby needs consistent, thought-out management to curtail bad habits. Parents must make a transition, too.

A Gradual Approach

Chapter 12 describes a dramatic, quick way to cure well-established sleep problems in children over six months old. In this chapter I would like to propose a more gradual approach to be tried in infants three, four, or five months old, right after the colic seems to have eased.

These are sensitive months in the development of a baby's crying and sleep patterns. In infants under three months, crying comes directly out of biological needs—for food and fluid, dry skin, contact and comfort, and in the case of colic, for relief from the unknown distress. Babies this young will not be spoiled or taught bad habits by your response to their crying. Infants over six months old, by contrast, can indeed learn to cry in order to get their parents to do certain things. They have learned to cry for attention. And they may have learned how to keep themselves from falling asleep. These interim ages—three, four, and five months—are a time to keep bad habits from forming and a promising time to teach a previously colicky, potentially sleepless baby how to stop crying and get enough rest. Remember, parents should be teachers!

The "Fade-Out" Procedure

I am going to give you some suggestions on how to do this. Basically, you will gradually decrease the amount of work you do when you put your baby to sleep. The goal is to let him develop internal resources to fall asleep. At the same time, you will be teaching yourself how to be the parents of a normal baby who does not always need your immediate attention.

Each family is different. Babies become ready at different ages. Please think of these suggestions as general principles rather than firm, tested rules. But do try to understand the basic theory: gradually, consistently cut back on the elaborate procedure you go through to get your child to sleep, until he is "weaned" from your company, and can do it on his own.

Step 1: Don't Pick Him Up

Your baby is now three to four months old. His colic is not as bad as it once was, but he still awakens frequently at night. Begin by figuring out how often your baby is truly hungry at night. Ask yourself how often he really sucks with enthusiasm. Listen to the quality of the crying—true hunger crying in the older infant has a sound all its own. Calculate how much time has passed since the last feeding: if it is less than two hours your baby could not possibly be hungry.

Now that you have decided how often you should feed your baby at night, pick him up and feed him at those times but do not pick him up at any other times. This is the first step: do not pick the baby up unless you are going to feed him.

Do you just ignore his cries? No. Go into his room and sit beside him. Pat him, stroke him, or hold his hand. Let him see you, and let him see you looking at him. Talk or sing. Keep it calm and gentle. Stay beside him as long as necessary, even until he falls asleep. Respond promptly each time he cries—but *do not* pick him up unless it is time for a feeding.

If your baby persists with inconsolable screaming despite your soothing efforts, stop. Go back to what method(s) you were using before. Try this suggestion again in a few weeks. Once you are able to calm him down, and pick him up only for feeding, move on to Step 2.

Step 2: Cut Back on Your Responses

Begin to cut back on what you do as you sit beside your baby. You might give up the eye contact first, keeping the room black and staying out of view. Later, stop rocking the crib or stroking the baby. Go slowly, see what works. The goal, after a week or two, is to reach the stage where you are merely resting your hand on the baby's back or quietly holding his hand. You still respond promptly and take as much time as necessary to lull him into a deep sleep. Pay attention to how much time this usually takes, and proceed to Step 3.

Step 3: Spend Less Time

Try to reduce, by a minute or two at a time, the amount of time you sit with your baby. Respond promptly, but slip away a little sooner. If you find that he startles and cries when you leave, go right back. After several days or a few weeks, you may find that just putting your hand on his back for a few minutes magically induces sleep. That will be a good accomplishment: You will have loosened the connection your baby used to make between long, complex social interactions and falling asleep. Now he may do it with only a quick reassurance of your presence.

Step 4: Wait a While

Now, for the first time, wait a bit before you go to the baby. Give him a chance to settle down by himself. Do not wait so long that a full crying storm develops, for then he will need a lengthy calming down. Wait two or three minutes to start, wait longer when you feel you can. Learn to recognize the drowsy, testing cries and wait them out. Your reward will come on those nights when you hear a call, some whimpering, a faint cry, and then silence.

Will It Work?

You need not take all these steps. If, for example, you had success with Steps 1, 2, and 3, but find that your baby always develops crying fits when you try Step 4, stop where you are. You have already made fine progress. Live with those brief nocturnal visits a few months more until the child outgrows this dependence on your presence. Sometimes this procedure works only when the father responds to the night awakenings and proceeds through Steps 1 through 4.

If this plan does not work at all for you, make sure you and your husband, and whoever else might tend to the baby at night, are all being consistent. You should always know how you plan to deal with the baby at night, and you should not give in, for example, pick him up, "just this once." It is also possible that your child is not ready; try again in a few weeks. I cannot predict whether this "fade-out procedure" will work for a particular family, but it is based on tested principles and I feel certain it is worth a serious try.

Chapter 11

There *Is* Life After Colic

*Mothers' Descriptions of Their Babies
at Age Four Months*

As part of a continuing study on colicky infants, I had the opportunity to study the parents' responses to the Infant Temperament Questionnaire (see Chapter 6), filled out when the infants were about four months old. Several mothers included a narrative account of the changes they had seen and I quote from these below. None of these infants was in my practice; I had not given any advice or counseling to these mothers. All the infants had colic as defined by Wessel, and the colic had disappeared by the time the parents filled out the questionnaire.

These comments from mothers of different backgrounds and circumstances illustrate the variety of ways colic can resolve itself. As you read on, you will see that behavior during the colicky period makes babies appear as alike as peas in a pod. There is not much individuality among screaming babies, especially to their exhausted mothers. However, the children outgrow this awful period with vastly different temperaments. I hope you have a dream baby at four months!

"He's Come a Long Way"

"With the colicky months behind us, I find Jacob very enjoyable and really no problem at all. Jacob has really come a long way from two months ago. He went from being a crying, crabby baby to a basically happy baby. His routine is, for the most part, regular. He tends to be a bit cranky around the dinner hour, but is calmed with picking up or just being in the middle of the activity. He enjoys being right in the middle of everything and everyone, and is up quite a bit. He gets excited watching his brother and sister play. He gets really excited and laughs when he plays with Daddy. If he's crabby and squirming, you know he's either wet or sleepy or it's time to eat. On the whole, I would say he is a fairly content little guy!"

"He Became a New Baby"

"At almost three months to the day, I felt Daniel was over his colic. He became a new baby with long times of playing and watching and seemed very happy. He suddenly established a routine of sleeping, eating and being awake. He followed it faithfully if me or my husband were the ones taking care of him. With anyone else, the routine of sleep was shortened and awake times lengthened, so he'd be fussy at the end, but it is amazing what a happy baby he has become. The only times that are still rather difficult are when he is in a car seat. When I hold him in the back of the van he is perfectly content. However, I drive a small car and then he is in a car seat, which proves to be distressing. Daniel does not take a pacifier on his own and will spit it out unless I help hold it. Rarely does he keep the pacifier in for more than sixty seconds if he's fussy, and he does not suck his thumb or fingers in place of the pacifier. Before with colic he needed constant attention and there was no solution to his crying. Now he is becoming a happy person. Fussiness now means specific problems: diaper, food, sleep, etc."

Daniel's mother, a thirty-two-year-old teacher, described her baby as not sucking very much. Brazelton reported that crying and sucking behavior were inversely related to each other. That is, crybabies do not suck very much and thumbsuckers do not cry very much.

"She Can Focus Her Energy Instead of Crying"

"Katherine's colic varied widely from day to day. On a good day there might have been only two to three hours of mild fussiness in the evening. She took naps, sleeping perhaps four hours during the day. She _always_ slept from midnight to 7:00 A.M. There were several play periods of twenty to forty minutes, and she certainly was fun! On bad days the colic lasted from six to eight hours, most of it in the moderate category, maybe an hour or two really severe. On these days, she was unable to sleep during the day. She would fall asleep but awaken a few moments later. Holding, rocking, and the pacifier helped, but she was unusually jumpy. The sound of my breathing startled her, for example. She still had some play periods after eating, but they were much shorter and less frequent. I ended up holding her most of the day. In an average week she had three bad days. One of the fussy days was due to her first DPT shot. I also noticed that on bad days, she looked pale and there was some perspiration on her forehead _before_ she began crying. I could sometimes tell ahead of time that she was going to have problems."

At about four months: "In general, Katie has had less severe colic, fewer hours of colic, and has slept more. It has been easier to get her to sleep and easier to keep her asleep. Her play periods are longer, and it's been interesting to watch her focus her energy on looking, reaching, batting and feeling things instead of having it tied up in crying. There has been only one instance of severe colic since, and it was short. She still has some "jittery" times, but on the whole they seem less severe. She still tends to have at least one very active period in the evening during which she energetically leaps, smiles, frowns, coughs, burps, widens her eyes and so on. However, she is less apt to disintegrate into screaming. More often, she falls into a light sleep and the rapidly changing facial expressions and panting continue for a few moments. Then she either awakens in a quieter mood or goes into a sound sleep."

The comments regarding panting are interesting because many mothers noted that just prior to the onset of colic the babies might breathe rapidly and with shallow respirations. Other mothers noted deep or labored breathing, like rapid sighs, just before the colic occurred. These changes in breathing patterns were previously reported by Wessel. Perhaps smooth muscle contractions in the lung are causing increased resistance to breathing similar to what occurs in asthmatics. The comment regarding *perspiration* or *pallor* before the crying started has not been previously reported, but perspiration was noted in the following mother's report.

"She Fights Sleep"

"My four-month-old infant, Marjorie, cries and fusses after her bath almost always for two to five minutes. She fights sleep continuously (one to two hours), rejects the last bottle, stiffens her body and when held pushes away from me by bending her legs, passing gas and her body perspires. Rocking, being held, played with, walked, etc. does not stop her shrill crying. The difficulty in the evenings has left me feeling that either she is spoiled or I'm not following a schedule properly and am promoting this overtired, extremely fussy period myself. Marjorie has been this way for ten weeks, but in the past six weeks she's become even more difficult to get to sleep."

"Cries Herself to Sleep"

"Tai is strong-willed, yet usually agreeable. She laughs and smiles very easily and is not fearful of strangers. She generally has a very good disposition. She is very inquisitive and very vocal. Tai frequently moves her arms and legs vigorously when playing with toys. She is very affectionate and generally likes to be held. When tired and fighting sleep, Tai becomes much more difficult. Even when she falls asleep while nursing she usually awakens when put into her crib and cries vigorously [i.e., red face, with tears and perspiration] for five to fifteen minutes until she falls asleep. Tai rarely sleeps longer than four hours at a time. During the daytime, naps range from thirty minutes to two and a half hours. She usually awakens from naps more calmly than she did a month or so ago. That is especially true if she has slept for a longer period of time.

"During the night, Tai usually sleeps for about four hours and awakens whimpering or crying. She is easily calmed by holding and nursing and falls asleep readily. When returned to her crib, however, she almost always cries for a few minutes before settling down to sleep. She does not cry if she is nursed in our bed and not moved."

"Very Opinionated"

"Charles has definitely calmed down, but is still very active during the day. He sleeps well all night, but does not want to take naps during the day. When colic was bad, it was at its worst during the day, no matter what I did. He is very opinionated as to what he'll eat and has lost interest in his bottle already. He still gets spurts of gas once in a while."

What Mothers Say About First Babies After Colic

Here are some young mothers describing their firstborn babies after they've grown out of a bout of colic.

"He Doesn't Sleep Like Other Children"

"David is a happy boy in general. He loves to take baths and kick in the tub. He also loves to have his hair brushed, his body rubbed with lotion, nails cut, ears cleaned, nose cleaned, etc. David is *big* on eating—anything he can suck—he still sucks his thumb when sleeping. He loves to be put on the changing table to dress and have his diaper changed. And he loves to be talked to! He is very friendly towards everyone and smiles and coos a lot. David is just great when we take him out—stores, houses—loves all the new things. He is easily stimulated by sights and sounds. David still doesn't sleep like other children, as long, that is, but he does sleep seven to eight hours each night, and one hour in the morning and one hour in the afternoon for naps, which sure beats being up every two hours!"

"I Feed Her Very Often"

"It is very hard, even impossible, to put Stephanie on a feeding schedule. When I do feed my child she *never* eats. I'm talking about nursing her more than ten minutes total, so I don't think she's very full. I find myself feeding her frequently. She gets very, very angry sometimes and will scream, and sometimes I can't tell if she might be in extreme pain."

"Nights Are Still Difficult"

"Previously, Matthew's colic could be descibed as moderate in nature with a total duration of about six hours each day—usually three hours in the early morning (3:00 A.M. to 7:00 A.M. or so), 11:00 A.M. to noon, and 4:00 P.M. to 6:00 P.M., and sometimes again between 9:00 P.M. and midnight. He usually had about ten wakings between midnight and 9:00 A.M. One rocking movement that he often responded to when crying intensely was an elevator-like movement—up and down on his back. However, this is physically demanding and can't be done for long. Now, his general behavior pattern is characterized by pleasantness. Matthew smiles most of the day and maintains the ability to charm, play and coo. However, night wakings are continually a problem. For the last three weeks he has awakened every hour."

"Demands a Lot of Attention"

"I have noticed marked improvements in Jonathan's behavior during his fourth month. Since his colic pains have subsided, he seems to be enjoying what life has to offer. However, when he gets tired of a certain activity (play, bath, swing, etc.), he is *very* impatient and screams continuously until I pick him up and move on to something else. I can't coax him to stay with a task if he doesn't want to. He is at a point now where he is showing a lot of emotion. He smiles and giggles out loud for long periods of time but he can cry two minutes later because he wants a change of activity. Jonathan demands a lot of attention and I wonder if this is because of when he had colic. Dinner is a difficult time because Jonathan does not like to sit and amuse himself while we eat. This is a problem we are still working on. Maybe this is true with many children. This being my first child, I'm not sure what is typical behavior but I would consider his temperament to be more difficult than average since he demands so much attention."

"She's Usually Calmer"

"Annie has a generally sunny disposition and is extremely gregarious. She does have strong negative reactions to things she's not ready for like dressing or being put to bed. When she was younger, Annie seemed to overreact to stimulation and had many more fussy periods. She still reacts strongly, but not necessarily negatively, and is usually calm."

"Dependency Is a Problem"

"Nelida has a very high level of activity and expresses her emotions through her physical movements. She seems to prefer communication through body language rather than vocal expression. When she vocalizes it's more through a demanding cry rather than cooing and being pleasant. She's a very alert, attentive child with good concentration and attention span, especially when her energy is at its peak in the evening. Being with us makes her feel secure and it is essential for her becoming sociable and outgoing. This has developed into a problem because her attachment and dependency has developed to such a degree that Nelida refuses to develop independence, or allow us to have ours."

Secondborn Infants Are Like
Firstborns After Colic

Secondborn children who have had colic are described in terms similar to those used by mothers of firstborn infants.

"Requires a Lot of Sleep"

"Elizabeth is only getting a formula for feedings—no solids. Four eight-ounce bottles keep her full. Her sleeping patterns and preferences are giving us the most problems. She requires a lot of sleep and is only awake six to seven hours a day. The problem is she will only sleep on her stomach in a crib. Sleeping in cribs other than her own also shortens her naps. She does not particularly enjoy stroller rides or car seats and never falls asleep in them. Her favorite activities involve being with other people. She enjoys being held, walked, talked to and played with. We are trying to encourage longer play periods alone. It's hard to take her places. She requires a lot of holding and walking."

"No Two Days Alike"

"Scott's behavior varies from day to day. It seems there are never two days in a row that are alike. He does follow something of a schedule for eating and sleeping but his behavior during waking hours changes a lot. He can almost always be comforted by holding."

"No Problem At All"

"At first, Nathaniel's crying was a problem because I didn't feel emotionally strong enough to handle it. A three-month span of colic seemed like it would be forever to me. We had trouble taking him visiting because right after supper time (about 7:30 P.M.) he would start to cry and wouldn't quit. No one could understand why he would suck a bottle and scream like it was hurting him. Once he got wound up he had a hard time relaxing and calming down. Things got better on the Bentyl. That medication was a real lifesaver. Now his temperament is no problem at all. I enjoy him, I think he's a cute baby. Maybe I'll have a third sometime!"

"I Can See More and More How to Help Her"

"Although Lauren has greatly improved since the time of her colic, she can't relax in her environment. If she ever must wait for something, especially a nap or feeding [milk] she will begin by fussing and then dissolve into tears. If this occurs around naptime she will take about twenty minutes to settle herself down, during which time there must be no stimulation at all. If she fusses at feeding time she will generally refuse the breast. The only solution is to place her in the crib and let her cry it out, the end result being a short nap, after which she wakes up cheerful and ready to eat.

"However, Lauren more than makes up for these angry out-bursts by being a very responsive child. She smiles a lot, freely giving belly laughs. She especially loves playing with me and her older sister. She can maintain cheerful play for up to an hour and sometimes more after a feeding. Her motor development is very good. One thing I've noticed is that she doesn't sleep well anywhere but in her own crib—she's very aware of changes in bed. For example she won't fall asleep in a restaurant in a car bed, but she can sometimes sleep in a snuggly. It feels good to see the light at the end of the tunnel. I can see more and more how to help Lauren over her sometimes very difficult irritability. I'm feeling much better about our relationship."

Experienced Mothers and Colicky Babies

Experienced mothers with two or three previous children may also experience a colicky baby.

"A Joy to All of Us"

"Before, Michael would scream and cry for hours and nothing we did seemed to help him. We would rock him, walk with him and he would still scream. He even fought the bottle. This would go on for four or five hours straight; then he'd fall asleep and sleep for approximately an hour, then start all over again. We didn't know what to do to pacify him because nothing seemed to help, and we felt sorry for him because we hated to see our son like that and not be able to help him. Once Michael started sitting up, it relieved him somewhat and now he is a very happy and content baby boy. He smiles, goos and coos and is starting to sleep more, and it seems to be a peaceful sleep. When he is awake now he is content and doesn't have to be held, rocked or walked constantly. He is a joy to all of us."

"Tremendous Difference"

"David seems to be very content in whatever we do with him; he also is very content on where we lay him down, observes everything quietly and amuses himself by watching the mobile in his crib. He also accepts changes in his routine very well. It's a tremendous difference from when he had colic."

*   *   *

Perhaps you will recognize in these descriptions of children during and after colic some of the things that your child is going through. Be comforted. This is all very typical. As these testimonials show, even the fussiest children outgrow colic. Some turn into dream babies; others continue to be more assertive, but all become much more responsive, predictable, and easy to live with.

Labeling your child's crying as colic tends to emphasize her worst behavior. Her good behavior is just as much a part of her personality. Closely observe your baby at her best, her worst, when awake and when asleep. Treasure the beautiful, smiling moments. This is your preview of the baby you may be living with soon.

Chapter 12

Postcolic Sleep Problems

There is, as we have seen, a significant coincidence between colic and later sleep problems. Not all colicky babies become poor sleepers, though, and not all babies with sleep problems went through a period of colic. So let's look at infant sleep disorders in a more general way. This will be useful to all parents who are bothered by their children's sleeping patterns.

What Is a Good Night's Sleep?

We do not know what sleep is for. That is, we do not understand the biological function of sleep. Some say that sleep evolved to prevent our prehistoric ancestors from hurting themselves bumping around in the dark!

The restorative power of sleep is a medical mystery. Ideally, sleep makes us feel at peace with ourselves and the world. However, some adults observed in a sleep laboratory said they did not feel restored or rested even after appearing to sleep well.

When their brain wave activity was analyzed, it sometimes appeared distorted. Apparently the quality of sleep is as important as the quantity. The brain is not simply a chemical battery that is recharged by sleep.

We cannot ask babies if they have had a good night's sleep. We know nothing about qualitative differences in babies' sleep patterns. We do know that tired parents, kept awake because their crybaby is screaming, cannot easily function as loving mothers and fathers. A sleeping problem for your baby means a sleeping problem for you. You will be encouraged to know that many infant sleep disorders can be modified.

Does Your Baby Have a Sleep Problem?

Sometimes it is hard to tell if there is a sleep problem. Most mothers do not mind getting up a few times at night to feed their babies during the first few weeks. Typically, these babies awaken once or twice and immediately fall asleep after a 10 to 15 minute feeding. By several weeks many babies awaken only once. Consider yourself fortunate if your baby sleeps this well. Not all infants do.

One mother of a colicky infant told me that she had fantasies of having just one night of uninterrupted sleep. She could not remember, she said, when she last felt rested. In the playground, when other mothers talked about their babies rolling over or sitting up, she talked only about her baby not sleeping. She wanted to attack those mothers whose children slept through the night; what had they done to deserve such luck? Her baby was several months old and still got up frequently every night and seemed never to want to sleep.

There was a sharp edge of desperation in the mother's request for help. She was almost out of patience waiting for the baby to outgrow this problem. We discussed how sleep patterns relate to awake behaviors, and how her baby had developed her sleep problem. After an extended explanation she knew what the problem was and how to solve it. This chapter will give you that explanation and treatment plan for your baby's sleeping problem.

What's Enough Sleep for a Newborn?

Sleep patterns in the newborn and during the first few months of life develop in a predictable fashion. During the first few days of life, there does not seem to be much individual stability regarding the duration of sleep time. That is, some babies change from being good sleepers to bad sleepers and back again. However, between six and thirty-three months of age, the total sleep duration, and longest sleep period usually were observed to be stable individual characteristics. Individual infants who are brief duration sleepers tend to remain that way. In this respect, sleep duration is like crying behavior and temperament—it shows little consistency at first, but after a few months it develops into a moderately stable individual characteristic. There are no significant sleep duration differences between boys and girls.

What Determines How Much a Baby Sleeps?

It is generally thought that the emergence of sleep patterns in the first few months is due to neurophysiological changes in the brain as it matures. Most of these changes occur in an orderly and predictable fashion. The duration of sleep decreases. The pattern in the sequence of sleep states changes with age.

The three- or four-month birthday appears to be an important milestone for sleep development. After this point, infants' sleep patterns tend to resemble those of adults. The normal adult periodic organization of sleep state patterns, the cycling from quiet non-REM sleep to active REM sleep, emerges at about *four months of age* and stays that way for the rest of an individual's life.

Contrary to popular belief, sleep duration is not influenced by introducing solid foods. Slipping a little cereal into that nighttime bottle will not really help. This fact has been documented in several studies where parents kept careful daily records of feeding and sleeping patterns. In France, there was a study of a group of infants who were never hungry. Because of birth defects involving their intestine or stomach, these infants were fed continuously through their veins. Even when their hunger rhythms were suppressed, the sleep-wake patterns remained unchanged. In other words, older infants wake up because their brain, not their stomach, turns on an alarm clock. Of course the infant will drink or nurse if offered the opportunity, but this is probably only to encourage the parent to stay a little longer. This nonnutritive or recreational snacking in the middle of the night is a form of social interaction that soothes the baby back to sleep, but older infants learn quickly that if they don't suck when offered the opportunity, even if not hungry, then their mother or father will more quickly put them down and leave.

Do breastfed babies awaken more often than bottlefed babies? Two studies on this subject, one of which was mine, reached opposite conclusions. However, there is no doubt that switching from breast to bottle or giving a supplemental bottle at night does not help babies *consistently* sleep through the night.

A widely quoted study showed that the twenty-four-hour sleep durations of individual infants were not influenced by the behavior of their caretakers. In other words, the total amount of sleep a baby got in a twenty-four-hour period seemed to be a constant. But the study did find that caretaking activity could influence the *length* of the longest single sleeping period, indicating that some biological rhythms might not be based on physiologic clocks, but rather learned early in life. Parents may function as time-givers: (1) parent-enforced scheduling of feeding and sleep times, and (2) promptness in their responses to an infant's needs may play a role in the child's developing day/night rhythms.

Night Wakings Are Normal

Awakenings at night are common in healthy infants, perhaps more common than their parents realize. Videotaping of infants at home has shown that they often awaken and return to sleep without calling out or crying. Brief episodes of night waking may reflect the physiological sleep rhythms occurring at night. We know that during the non-REM state, sleep alternates between deep sleep and light sleep. In some children, the "light" stage is probably so light that they awaken partially or completely. This is not a problem unless it regularly disturbs the parents or keeps the child from getting enough sleep. As he grows, a child should develop his own resources to return to sleep without his parent's help.

In one study of over one hundred infants, researchers focused on awakenings accompanied by crying or fussing between midnight and 5:00 A.M. which occurred at least once a week. By age three months, 70 percent of the babies had no night awakenings. By age six months, 83 percent of all babies were sleeping through the night, and by one year of age 90 percent of babies slept through the night. Again it should be noted that settling, or no night waking, was not related to the sex of the baby, birth weight, or weight at age three months. Also, the mother's personality did not appear to influence night waking.

Boy-Girl Differences

A study of night waking using home videotape measurements observed that male infants had more irregular sleep schedules than females. Our study at the Children's Memorial Hospital also showed that parents perceived night waking to be a problem in their sons more often than in their daughters. Therefore, night waking as a problem—unlike colic or difficult temperament problems—might be a bit sex-specific.

Parental Response

In one study infants who cried more and infants who slept less (twenty-four-hour accumulated total) tended to have more night wakings.

In another study the mothers' behavior toward the night waking was divided into three patterns: always feeding, never feeding, and sometimes feeding. The group of babies fed "sometimes," described in the study as receiving inconsistent handling, had significantly more awakenings.

It seems that inconsistent parental responses to night waking in older infants may encourage the habit, magnify the problem, lead to more crying at night and more difficulties in the infant returning to sleep. This pattern is referred to as "trained night crying," and may be a common sequel to colicky behavior.

When Older Babies Wake at Night

Interestingly, about half of all infants who settled before five months of age will begin night waking between six and twelve months. Many mothers have asked me, "What am I doing wrong? Why is he getting me up now after sleeping through the night these past months?" Perhaps the baby is now more curious and attentive to his surroundings.

Night waking is a very common problem in older babies. Up to 40 percent of mothers describe problems in putting their child to sleep or problems in having him sleep through the night. If your child has a sleeping problem, you are not alone.

I advise mothers of older babies to be *consistent* in their response to night waking. During the first few months, always respond promptly to your baby's crying. After four, five, certainly six months, it is time to change your tactics. Begin by trying to analyze whether there is any special reason for your baby waking at night.

Why Older Children Awaken

Breathing Difficulties

Some infants and older children awaken frequently throughout the night because they have difficulty breathing during sleep. These children may habitually snore. They may breathe through their mouths when asleep and awake. Their breathing may appear labored when they are asleep. During the day these children appear either very sleepy or all wound up with nervous energy. When these children awaken at night it is not a behavioral problem, it is a physiological problem. Consult your pediatrician immediately if you think your child has this condition.

Nightmares and Night Terrors

These are unique kinds of waking at night. They are each different. A child who has had a nightmare is agitated, excited, and can remember and tell about a frightening dream. He may easily awaken or awaken spontaneously; can be consoled quickly and return to sleep. Night terrors also involve great agitation. In some cases the child appears to be afraid and wild-eyed, but has no memory of a bad dream. He cannot be easily awakened or easily soothed.

Both nightmares and night terrors occur more commonly when a child has a fever. Every child will probably suffer from one or the other every once in a while. If your child frequently awakens in fright, you should consult your pediatrician and perhaps a child psychologist.

Low Sensory Threshold

Many infants who awaken frequently at night have a low sensory threshold. As we pointed out earlier, they are more easily startled or awakened by ordinary noises, vibrations, drafts, or light. If you suspect your child is unusually sensitive this way, reduce external stimulation at night. I will describe how later on.

The Wrong Sleep Schedule

Frequent night awakening sometimes seems to stem from an inappropriate sleep schedule. As we discussed in Chapter 7, the body has its own internal rhythms which ideally are in synchrony with deep sleep, light sleep, and wakefulness.

In one instance, a child who had had colic as an infant would awaken three or four times each night—sometimes for several minutes, sometimes for over an hour. All my tricks to help this family failed until we decided to shift the child's sleep schedule. We awakened her about seven o'clock in the morning and did not allow her to begin naps after 11 in the morning. Instead of staying up until an abnormally late hour, usually 11:00 P.M. or midnight, she was put to bed at nine. Two improvements occurred immediately. First, the time required to put the child to sleep decreased from about forty-five minutes to five. Second, the number of night awakenings, and the duration of each night awakening decreased dramatically. This child had simply been asked to sleep during the wrong hours.

This example suggests that an imposed sleep schedule which is out of sync with the child's biological rhythms (such as body temperature, hormone secretion, etc.) might distort sleep patterns. Healthy, restorative sleep might depend on timing the evening sleep onsets and morning awakenings, so that perhaps they can occur when the body's temperature and endocrine levels are right. Sleep scheduling might be as important as sleep duration.

Do not become enchanted by claims that babies simply fall asleep whenever they are tired, regardless of circumstances. Yes, there are infants who can nap in the stroller, at a party, in the car. But others never adapt to this kind of behavior. They do not rest well unless it is dark and quiet. Protect your baby's natural sleeping schedule. Do not try to force the baby to adjust her sleeping patterns to your lifestyle.

Parental Reinforcement

Parents often unintentionally contribute to their child's bad sleep habits. This is particularly true when the baby has been colicky and the parents have gotten used to rocking and walking with him. When the child continues to want this attention at night, the parents don't realize they are reinforcing a bad habit. Often they are on "automatic pilot": it is 3:00 A.M., they are half asleep and all they know is that they must promptly attend to the baby or the crying will surely get worse.

The same thing might happen during the day. Older infants who awaken frequently at night also take abnormally brief naps. The baby loses sleep and the mother misses an opportunity to catch up on her own rest. Often these babies would learn to take longer naps if they were not picked up from their cribs at the first whimper.

Your Cranky Child May Just Be Tired

Some parents, especially parents whose children have been colicky, seem unable to tell when their babies are simply exhausted. Mothers often tell me that their infants do not need as much sleep as other infants. They report, no doubt accurately, that their babies never rub their eyes, yawn, put their heads down, or appear to be tired. These mothers don't realize that short-tempered, irritable, hyperactive behavior is also a sign of fatigue. Some mothers use the fact that their child occasionally falls asleep in stores, parks, or other noisy places as "proof" that the child has no sleep problem. On the contrary, this could mean that the infant has become so totally exhausted that he simply conks out.

Sleep deprivation affects *mood* much more than it does activity. We see this in adults who as part of an experiment reduced their nightly sleep duration. They were usually able to function well the next day. As long as they get about five hours of sleep a night, they can complete tasks, show adaptive physical skills, and appear to be quite capable of thinking through problems. But they feel awful. They report feeling slightly or very ill. Their temperament changes radically. So imagine the effect of insufficient sleep on a young child.

A good way to tell whether your child is getting enough sleep is to observe how he behaves when awakening. Babies who are sleeping enough are pleasant and playful; babies who never get enough rest awaken crying and grimacing and appear to be uncomfortable for no apparent reason. Remember that fussy, overactive behavior is as clear an indication of fatigue as is yawning or dozing off. It is not true that infants simply doze off whenever they are tired. Many need help in getting themselves to sleep.

Treatment of Trained Night Crying

Let the Baby Alone

The best way to manage trained night crying in an infant over four or five months of age is to consistently leave him alone at night, even if he cries. This always works. Within a few days you will see a reduction in the frequency and duration of nighttime crying spells. Before long your baby will learn to sleep through the night.

Learn to Be Consistent

Consistency is the key to breaking this habit. Parents who have been through the ups and downs and twists and turns of colic may find this a big change. For as long as you have known this baby, you have had to be flexible; now you must make an about-face and be consistent. Please believe that your baby is ready for a routine, even if he has never been in the past. Realize that you have a few habits of your own to change: you will have to stop letting the baby "call the tune." *You* will now set the schedule, and let the baby cry until he sleeps. You will have to harden your heart a tiny bit, after months of flooding your baby with sympathy and prompt attention. Once you and he make the transition your life will be easier and more predictable and, believe me, your baby will be happier too. But you are going to have to teach yourselves a new pattern of parenting.

Reduce External Stimulation

For the child who had colic and/or is very stimulus sensitive, reducing the amount of external stimulation helps the child go to sleep.

Begin by modifying the child's bedroom. To get the room completely dark, mount opaque blackout shades on the outer molding of the window and hold them in place with curtains, tape, or picture framing. Obviously, there should be no night light and the door should be almost completely closed. If you need to cool the room with a window air-conditioner, run it before the infant goes to bed and turn it off when he sleeps. Keep the windows closed to eliminate street noises. You might cover central air ducts to reduce the clicking on and off noises of the heating or air conditioning system. A steady background noise from a vaporizer, humidifier, or "white noise" machine might help drown out intermittent sounds. Of course, you should not run the garbage disposal, dishwasher, or vacuum cleaner during nap time. If possible, turn the telephone off or cover it with a pillow. Do not go into the child's room or even open his door to peek in.

Crib toys and accessories should be removed except for one special security blanket or doll. The bedroom is a place to sleep; it is not a playground.

Making your child's room pitch dark and quiet should be thought of as only a temporary measure. You will not make your child permanently dependent upon these conditions in order to sleep. In the future, you will be able to have dinner parties and go on vacations and your child will sleep. A remarkable change occurs when your baby sleeps well for several weeks or months in a peaceful environment. Gradually, the child appears less jumpy, less irritable, less restless, and more able to attend to one thing at a time. This overall decreased behavioral responsiveness suggests a decrease in the state of arousal, which probably results from the change to better-quality sleep or sleep that is uninterrupted and prolonged. Now that the child is better rested, he is less likely to fight going to sleep and he is less likely to be thoroughly awakened when the telephone rings or the garage door opens. He still may be a light sleeper, compared to other children, but he won't behave as if his nervous system was always excitable.

Begin with Bedtime

Maintain a regular sleep schedule, with bedtime and wake-up time at the same hours every day. Establish nighttime rituals and stick to them. Fathers should be involved in these rituals and should sometimes place the child in bed after the mother has nursed. Read a book or sing the same medley of songs every night. Make bedtime a happy time; do not act as though you expect a struggle, do not make going to bed seem like a punishment.

Children will learn to fall asleep (or fall back asleep if they wake later) because it is dark, quiet, and boring in the bedroom alone. Once you start leaving the child alone at night, do not relent. The goal is to teach her that she will get no further companionship from you until morning.

Parents: No Excuses!

Pediatricians have a hard time convincing parents that it is all right to leave a baby alone and let her cry. Sometimes a father who is the only wage-earner demands that the mother quiet the child so that he can get his rest. Mothers also worry about disturbing other people: children, resident in-laws, or neighbors.

Sometimes parents are afraid of hurting their baby's feelings or making him angry. They are supported in this fear by a number of popular infant-care books which say that leaving a child to cry will make him feel abandoned, give him a complex, and cause him to resent you forever. In my opinion, it is absurd to believe that a few hours of crying will undo the thousands of hours of love, tenderness, and security that you give your baby. Children are very resilient; their psyches are tough, they appear to forget quickly, and they do not carry grudges. You will find, I guarantee, that even when it has taken your little guy hours to cry himself to sleep, he will be cheerful, affectionate, and glad to see you in the morning. Anyway, this may be the first time but certainly will not be the last time in your child's life that you will have to do something for his good health which might seem to make him unhappy at the time. Prolonged uninterrupted sleep occurring on the right schedule is a health habit. You can teach sleep hygiene just as you would teach hand washing, teeth brushing, balanced diet, and so forth.

Occasionally parents have hidden conflicts which get in the way of their resolve. Perhaps a career woman simultaneously wants to stay at home and nurse her baby but also wants to return to work. Depending on how she is feeling at any given time, she may leave the child alone or she may rush to his side. This inconsistent behavior encourages the night awakening and crying.

Some mothers cannot let their child cry because they imagine some illness is causing the night awakening. They may exaggerate minor common colds or rashes. One family decided that their fourteen-month-old child was awakening early every morning because of a gastrointestinal problem. Undigested vegetable matter in the child's stools "proved" this. I examined the stools, reassured the mother that many healthy children have frequent loose stools, and told her that these same children often have sleep problems. When the family realized that the child would outgrow this chronic, nonspecific diarrhea and that it did not mean he had a disease, they focused their efforts on behaviorally managing the sleep problem by letting the child get himself back to sleep.

Another family blamed all nighttime problems on teething. From the age of six months on, the child was imagined to be constantly suffering from some painful tooth eruption. But, surprise! Letting this baby cry at night cured the teething pain for good.

Health professionals need to help parents avoid rationalizations and excuses. They should explain normal sleep development and at the same time help parents arrive at a reasonable plan for treatment, providing support as the plan is carried out. Warn the mother that she might feel she is being cruel, but emphasize that she is not punishing her child. She is teaching him a good health habit: sufficient, uninterrupted, restful sleep. Urge the family to call you frequently during the first few days; they will be needing your encouragement.

Make the Decision

Helping your child break a bad sleep habit is a major task. Fortunately, it is quickly accomplished, but it will be hard on you. It might be worth waiting until the parents can take time off from work. You may be up all night or get only fragments of sleep, and working during this time could be difficult, if not dangerous.

Be sure to discuss your plans with your other children. Explain to them that the baby will be crying at night because you are breaking a bad habit. Make sure your older children know that you are not punishing the baby and that he's not suffering.

Warn your neighbors if they are within earshot. Explain that the treatment will last only a few nights and will put an end to the nighttime crying which has probably been bothering them, too.

. . . And Then Do It

To break down your baby's associating falling asleep with being held, put him into his crib while he is still awake, then shut the door and *do not go back.*

Don't be surprised when the baby cries for a long time with great gusto the first couple of nights. She wants a return of the old style of parental attention and will put forth extra energy to that end. Remember that your baby will not hurt her lungs or vocal cords, choke, suffocate, or anything else. Do not become alarmed. Do not weaken. Do not peek into the bedroom; this will only recharge the baby's battery.

When the baby cries and cries the first night the mother should wear earplugs, take long showers, go into the basement or go for a walk. Dear mothers, get away from the crying! It will tear at your heart. Let your husband sit outside the door of the infant's room. Use your ingenuity: one family lived in a small house with no place to escape from the baby's crying. The father borrowed a friend's camper-van and parked it in the driveway at night. On alternate nights the parents took turns sleeping in the van so that one parent was always rested. Another family found that only if both parents stayed together could they give each other the strength to resist the temptation to rush to the baby's side. Do what works for you.

The typical sequence is for the baby to cry for several hours the first night, and to awaken frequently throughout the night. The second night there is a briefer initial crying period and fewer, briefer night awakenings. The parents usually note that the morning after the second night the child awakens later than usual. He is probably tired from two nights of strenuous crying. By the third night, there is substantially less crying. Many parents report that for the first time the child appears tired around the bedtime hour. Usually there are few to no awakenings by the fourth or fifth night.

If It Doesn't Work

If you let your baby cry according to these suggestions and you see no improvement after a few days, perhaps the child is too young. I have seen this plan fail (though rarely) in babies five and six months of age. However, by eight or nine months, when the parents try it again, it always works. I believe this four-day treatment is worth trying every three or four weeks from six months of age on.

Praise Improvement

When the parents succeed in encouraging regular sleep habits, the child becomes much easier to live with.

The increased rest for both child and parents makes a world of difference.

After several months without night awakenings, the parents can relax the strict routine somewhat. They can take trips with the child, cope with an illness (such as an ear infection) which interrupts sleep, and be less rigid in maintaining the sleep schedule when social activities occur. Once the special event or ear infection is over, the parents should resume their consistent regular handling and the child will again start sleeping through the night.

Sometimes, after several quiet months, the child starts to visit his parents at two or three in the morning, wanting company. Parents should not panic that the old problem is returning. Just escort him back to his room and briefly explain that this is not the way to behave. Then praise him on subsequent nights when he does not come calling, and thank him for not leaving his room. After a few days, the child will no longer bother the sleeping parents.

Drugs to Make Your Baby Sleep

I have saved discussion of sedative drugs for last because I do not believe they can solve behavioral problems. It has been my experience that parents view drugs as a quick fix and make no effort to change their behavior. Therefore, despite a few days of improvement, the problems continue. I don't think drugs play any role in the *permanent* management of trained night crying.

Still, medicine may be useful on a temporary basis in extreme cases to help disrupt an abnormal sleep schedule or to give parents a break so that they can gather their strength. Hypnotics, sedatives, the amino acid tryptophan and antihistamines are all sometimes prescribed to produce drowsiness. Only one clinical study has been performed on an antihistamine called diphenhydramine. This drug was given to fifty children between the ages of two and twelve. In a random fashion, some received the drug and some received a placebo; neither investigators, parents, nor patients knew who got which. After one week those patients started on placebo were switched to diphenhydramine, and vice versa. Parents kept detailed diaries of the children's sleep patterns during these two weeks. These diaries showed that the drug did significantly shorten the time it took children to fall asleep and decreased the number of awakenings per night. The patients were not studied beyond two weeks.

The problem with any drug, including diphenhydramine, is that the apparent benefit appears to diminish rapidly over a period of several days or a few weeks. And, of course, no parent should want her child taking drugs over a long period of time, especially when the problem could be handled better with common sense, will power, and lots of love.

Not All Night Waking Is a Problem

I want to emphasize that this approach —letting the baby cry as long as necessary—is appropriate only in the case of trained night crying. If your baby awakens at night only occasionally, if his fussiness comes from a verified fever or ear infection pain, if he seems to need comfort when there has been a change in his life—then, by all means, comfort him. He will not develop a bad habit if you go to him a few nights out of the month. Just be sure you are not using teething or "what happened during the day" as an excuse night after night. As Dr. Illingworth, the dean of infant crying research, wrote: "No baby should ever be left crying for prolonged periods—except when one is breaking a habit produced by mismanagement."

Chapter 13

"How We Taught Our Baby to Sleep"

Some Mothers Talk About Their Experiences

The cycle of exhaustion, fussiness, poor sleep habits, and sleep deprivation is a baffling one to families in the midst of it. On the surface, nothing seems terribly amiss, yet everything is wrong. Baby and parents reinforce each others' bizarre schedules. Other problems are blamed. Where there was colic, parents assume it mutated into new and equally distressing forms.

Following are accounts by some of the mothers who have consulted me for their children's sleep problems. All of these babies once had colic. I have quoted at length in order to convey the relentless, unpredictable nature of trained night crying. Some of these stories are bound to make any mother feel lucky by comparison. While they show how a sleep problem can get out of hand, and how it can masquerade as something else, they also show how easily it can be corrected once it is identified.

Here is a thirty-two-year-old mother with professional training. You'll notice that despite the professionals she consulted and all of the approaches she tried, no one addressed the issue of sleep, the most obvious problem.

Joel's Mother

"Looking back, my concern for Joel started in the hospital: the nurses said that he cried all the time in the nursery and would bring him to me for feeding and comforting—often at hourly intervals. I left the hospital exhausted. Since Joel is my only child, and I am an only child, I had little to compare him with. The first three months home were brutal and, although I suspected as much, I didn't admit until he was almost four months old, that his behavior wasn't 'normal.' I guess that is something no parent ever wants to see—or believe.

"Life with Joel during those months was disruptive and draining. He had no schedule, slept very little (maybe eight hours in a twenty-four-hour period, in one- to three-hour blocks) and cried a good deal of the time. Meeting Joel's needs filled my day; besides feeding him and changing him, the major task was keeping him quiet. Several things worked at different times: walking him in his infant seat, especially outside, while singing; car rides; visiting anywhere; carriage rides. We became vagabonds. Often a day would include several carriage rides, some lasting up to ninety minutes; a trip to the store; and a visit with a friend. After only five hours of interrupted sleep each night—I found it hard to get back to sleep. I'd be exhausted. But I couldn't stop moving.

"Bedtime for Joel was usually 10:00 P.M. We couldn't just put him in his crib. I had to rock him, walk him, nurse him, and lay him down ever so gently. He would usually wake up once during the process and we'd have to begin again. The process in total generally took an hour. I'd then fall into bed hoping I could unwind and get to sleep quickly, knowing that I'd be up two to three times that night and up for good at 5:00 to 5:30 A.M.

"I waited as patiently as I could for Joel to get his act together. I'd heard that at three to four months colicky babies miraculously became settled and slept through the night. At three months Joel did sleep through the night for approximately six days. A start, we thought, but it quickly ended.

"By Joel's four-month checkup, I was completely demoralized. I prayed he had an ear infection to explain his irritability and lack of sleep. When he was given a clean bill of health, I cried. The pediatrician suggested a sedative. When I filled the prescription the pharmacist told me that the medication was an antihistamine, one sometimes used to make a fussy baby go to sleep.

"I decided then to get a second opinion. Joel could *get* to sleep—he needed help *staying* asleep. I put the medication aside and headed for the telephone. Although I felt physically drained myself—hanging on by my fingertips, having to go on despite my physical exhaustion—my greatest anxiety was reserved for Joel. I wanted to help him. He was in discomfort and the world must have seemed a terrible place to him. I felt so responsible, yet unable to reckon with what I needed to do, and no one to tell me. He wasn't a colicky baby any more, but he cried a lot and couldn't be comforted. It was obvious that he wanted to sleep, but couldn't. I felt so helpless.

"The new pediatrician was supportive but gave few answers. Joel seemed healthy. We did detect a hip problem—though nothing painful enough to explain the poor sleeping pattern.

"During this time, I also contacted the local Birth to Three program for help. The child development specialist there felt that Joel was hypersensitive and irritable, lacked bilateral integration, and showed an uncharacteristic-for-his-age, strong preference for his right side. She agreed that Joel was different from other babies and might need a different approach. She gave recommendations for dealing with the motor delays, but seemed cool to the idea of 'letting Joel cry.' Joel also saw a physical therapist from Birth to Three who confirmed what the child development specialist saw. He suggested that the 'cause' could be just a developmental delay, a nervous system that wasn't quite ready to stabilize, or a mild brain injury that might or might not repair itself with time.

"Now I was busy with exercises for Joel's hip that the physical therapist recommended as well as other activities suggested by the Birth to Three specialists to help improve Joel's left side functioning and bilateral integration.

"No one addressed the issue of sleep. By the time Joel was eight months old, his irritability had decreased some but his sleep patterns had not improved. On the days he was rested, he was charming. In fact, even when he wasn't rested he could appear jovial and content—as long as we kept moving. At this time I issued an edict: no more night feedings. I'd feed Joel at 9:30 P.M., his bedtime, and at 5:00 A.M., his waking time, but not in between. I felt he was ready for this.

"My husband became Joel's 'walker.' Once to twice a night, he'd go to Joel and walk him back to sleep. The first few months of Joel's life had been mine, these next few were his father's. In the early months, it was 'Joel must be hungry,' or 'I have to go to work,' so Mother dealt with Joel. Now Mother bowed out and Dad finally began to believe that maybe something really was wrong with Joel. Mother didn't actually sleep more, but at least I spent more time in bed!

"Our marriage was really strained during Joel's first year. We couldn't take out our frustrations on Joel, so we took them out on each other. Looking back, some of my behavior was hysterical and irrational. My husband seemed to do a lot of denying. We both realized our behavior was related to physical exhaustion, but we seemed unable to reverse the direction.

"I saw an announcement in a local paper about an infant sleep disorders center. They sent me a questionnaire; I filled it out immediately. The questions made me think perhaps there were other children like Joel.

"At the center Dr. Weissbluth agreed that Joel was healthy. Joel, he said, just needed some sleep, and so did his parents. The fact that the doctor had seen other children like Joel, and that they had improved, was reassuring. The doctor's confidence in his procedure was encouraging, but did he really know Joel? I was hooked by the doctor's promise to follow up by phone to check Joel's progress during the course of the treatment to get Joel to sleep. I could scream at him if it didn't work and he could share the frustration.

"Something inside told me that at nine and one half months Joel was ready and I was ready too for his development. I liked the doctor's picture of my assuming a parenting role with Joel—not 'letting him cry' but 'teaching him to sleep,' letting him become independent and learning to get to sleep on his own.

"Anyway, we all were ready. And, with a few setbacks, it worked in two days. I believe it worked because Joel's system had matured. Could it have worked sooner? Joel was nine and one half months old. Maybe he was ready a month earlier, but earlier than that, I'm not sure.

"It helped us not only to be given permission to let Joel get himself to sleep in his own crib, but in fact to be told it was a parental responsibility. With a baby who slept through the night and napped twice a day, our lives not so much improved as began again. I feel we're normal now."

This distressing sequence of events is not uncommon. Nor is it uncommon that the mother tried everything, took all advice, drove herself frantic, even believed for a time that her son had a brain injury, when all they needed was sleep.

Another mother, a twenty-seven-year-old homemaker with a partial college education, described her experiences ("our ten-month ordeal") with her first daughter as follows:

Melissa's Mother

"My husband, Kevin, and I were blessed with a beautiful baby girl on June 13, 1981. We were so happy, but it was definitely a change in the household. I started breastfeeding and I wasn't very successful, so after two weeks Melissa was put on formula. I really don't think it was easy for Melissa to settle in. Two weeks after she was born we moved from an apartment into a house. It was a really chaotic time for all of us.

"After a month or so in the house we all felt better being settled in, but we became sure of one thing—Melissa had colic. She was not on any kind of schedule and the most she slept was about four hours at one time. This was not always consistent either. At this time we didn't consider her not sleeping too much of a problem. Being new parents, we weren't exactly sure how things were supposed to be or what we should do.

"After the colic stage was supposed to have ended we started worrying because Melissa still was not sleeping. Consulting her pediatrician on many occasions, we tried everything: different formulas, Donnatal, chamomile tea, warm clothes on her tummy,

Tylenol. We even tried the Rail Runner, a train put on the rail of her crib which played music and moved back and forth very slowly. Within fifteen minutes Melissa was supposed to be sound asleep. No luck.

"For ten months, nothing we did worked. During this time everyone had advice to give us. Some of the comments were: 'Maybe you just have a baby that won't sleep.' 'You are spoiling her by holding her all the time so she will sleep.' 'Just leave her in the crib and let her scream.' 'When she's ready she'll fall into a schedule.' I was so confused! Kevin and I would talk about the situation and our worry was that something was wrong with Melissa, even though she appeared to be a totally healthy baby.

"We loved her so much that we worked our schedules around Melissa. We both were like walking zombies. I would hold Melissa and give her a bottle so she might get an hour or two of sleep. As soon as I laid her in the crib she would start crying. At times I was so tired I would lay her next to me on our bed and pray for one hour of sleep. I would spend all day in my pajamas tending to Melissa. Since Kevin's sleep was more important due to a full time job, I would sleep when he got home from work for two to three hours and the rest of the time I would catnap when Melissa did. The longest period of time I was up without sleep was seventy-two hours. I had to call Kevin home from work because I couldn't stand up anymore.

"It was a physically and emotionally trying time for Kevin and myself. We argued a lot and we really weren't communicating with each other. We were both just too tired to even talk sometimes. We didn't have much of a love life, but it was our strong love for each other that held all three of us together. I would cry a lot and pray that soon Melissa would sleep.

"Melissa was so happy and good under the circumstances. I would look at her while she was awake and be amazed. 'How can she be so playful and alert? She's not getting enough sleep!' She even had dark circles under her eyes.

"Well, after ten months Kevin saw an excerpt on the news about sleep problems in children. We decided to get more information. I called and we were sent a questionnarie to fill out. Kevin and I felt this was our last hope.

"We talked with Dr. Weissbluth about Melissa and he checked her over. After our discussion he said that we had to put Melissa on a regular schedule. Even if she cried we had to leave her in the crib during naps and nighttime. We could use music and a fan, but had to make sure almost everything was out of her crib and the room was dark. He told us this procedure should show results in about seven days. I remember crying all the way home but Kevin reassured me that it was for Melissa's own good as well as ours.

"We started on a Friday night. Kevin stayed with Melissa and I went to stay at my mom's. I knew if I stayed home I would be in tears all the time and we probably wouldn't have gone through with it.

"It wasn't as bad as I had imagined. Kevin told me that Melissa cried for about forty-five minutes and then fell asleep. She also got up in the night and cried, but not for very long. He left her in the crib no matter what.

"After the first night she adapted very well. It was harder trying to get her to take a nap, but after about two to three weeks on constant reinforcement we had a baby who enjoyed sleeping. We would put her down for the night at 7:30 P.M., and she would sleep until 7:00 A.M. the next morning. Her naps would range from two to four hours, one nap a day. Believe me, we had a lot to celebrate on Melissa's first birthday!

"Now Melissa is sixteen months old. She cries in her sleep from time to time, due to teething or illness, but at least we know what is wrong and we can help her. We have a beautiful daughter who we love very much. Kevin and I can now enjoy a good night's sleep and peace of mind."

Another sensitive, intelligent thirty-eight-year-old mother went through a seventeen-month-long series of explanations for her son's problem before discoving it was a sleep disturbance. As you will see, she blamed hunger, the food she was eating, the medicine she was taking, the makeup she was wearing, flu, hyperactivity, teething, Tylenol, etc. Time and again she believed she had solved the problem, only to have it recur. Let me assure you, as the doctor who examined David, that despite the mother's harrowing descriptions of bloody stools, throwing up, bulging eyes, etc., there was never anything physically wrong with David. Please consider reading this account twice, first paying attention to how the baby behaved, then focusing on how the mother behaved.

David's Mother

"David is seventeen months old and for the first time I can honestly say I enjoy him and being a mother. With him sleeping through the night, I see a tremendous personality change. He has suddenly come alive and has taken a greater interest in his environment. He explores the outside rather than asking to be carried. He is no longer terrified of new situations and is beginning to interact with other children. He actually *sits down* and plays with his toys. Most important, he is now a happy, affectionate baby.

"I feel a very large load has been taken off of me. I know now it was David's colic and lack of sleep that affected his behavior, not my mothering. Up until now, no matter how I tried to convince myself otherwise, I was certain it was my fault.

"Why? Our first pediatrician considered David to be a 'well baby.' He was the type of doctor who believed a baby wasn't ill unless he had a terrible disease like cystic fibrosis. He never even suggested we might have a baby with colic. Through the first five miserable months, he repeatedly told us there was nothing wrong with David; he was gaining weight, therefore he was healthy.

"All I had to do was compare David with other babies his age and I knew there was something wrong. I assumed that it had to be my mothering. He was not comfortable enough to sleep during the day, sit in an infant seat or ride in a buggy without crying. He was up three times a night, each time for at least forty-five minutes. Whenever he was up he wanted to be held.

"He was so hungry that, initially, he rejected nursing. It took too long and he found it too difficult to suck. I remember feeling personally rejected when he refused to nurse, but I wanted to badly and continued to try. It took three weeks to get him to nurse without giving him a short drink from the bottle first. During that time he would scream before a feeding, drink for a short period, then scream again and double up with stomach cramps. I hung on, hoping the nursing would get better.

"The only information I had about nursing and a mother's diet during nursing was from books. Our pediatrician never offered any information or reasons for my child's behavior.

"It occured to me that perhaps what I was eating might be affecting David. I was eating prunes every day. Once I stopped the prunes, his cramps seemed to reduce and he was much more comfortable. He was then able to take one nap a day.

"When David was one month old, the 'flu' bouts started. I began to have flulike symptoms, diarrhea and severe cramps. The next day David would begin throwing up, having diarrhea with mucus and severe cramps. My flu lasted a few days each episode; his lasted exactly ten days. This occurred five different times before his three-month checkup. Each time, we called the pediatrician and he reassured us. As long as David wasn't dehydrated and had gained weight at his last checkup, the doctor said we shouldn't worry.

"I finally realized every time I ate chop suey, it seemed to make both of us sick. I had never reacted to Chinese food before but it seemed like the pregnancy and delivery changed my system. The MSG must have had a violent effect on both of us!

"During this time, I was becoming increasingly depressed. I was making my baby sick and feeling incredibly guilty about it. Many well-meaning friends and relatives urged me to stop nursing. I was hearing terrific comments like 'There must be something wrong with your milk,' or 'What have you been eating to make David sick again?'

"After David's three-month checkup, he began having screaming bouts that were so severe his eyes bulged. There was no way to comfort him. Also during this time, David's stools changed to dark green with mucus and traces of blood.

"Bill and I were very worried. We were tired of the platitudes coming from our pediatrician. When we pushed him for more help he suggested we take David in for an upper and lower G.I.

"It was obviously time to find a new doctor. Dr. K was referred by a friend. In my first telephone conversation with the new doctor, he asked me more questions than my first pediatrician did during the entire time he was treating David.

"We focused on my diet. I eliminated milk products and slowly stopped these foods I was eating on a daily basis that might affect David. Nothing seemed to help.

"Then the pediatrician questioned me about medication I might be using. I was taking an antihistamine for allergies. He suggested I stop for a few days because of the yellow dye. I seemed to have a new baby. His stools changed from green to yellow. He stopped screaming. He was calmer and happier. We were ecstatic. I very much wanted to believe everything would be fine.

"I started a new antihistamine with green dye. David reacted again, but this time worse than ever. I tried several white allergy medications until I found one that didn't make either one of us sick.

"At this point, my pediatrician suggested we read a book on hyperactive children. We didn't want to read it, but then David had a reaction to the dyes in children's Tylenol.

"When he was six months old, we gave him Tylenol for what we thought was teething pain. The pain got worse and we gave him more Tylenol. This continued until I realized his reactions were too severe to be teeth related. I couldn't hold him. He never stopped moving. He'd crawl down my leg, continuously squirm in my arms, bang his head against objects, grab at our faces and scream. As bad as his sleeping was before, it was now much worse. There were some nights when he was up for hours either staring into space or constantly moving.

"Bill and I read Feingold and were convinced he was writing about our baby. We tried to reassure ourselves that David wasn't seriously ill, but in our guts I don't think it really helped. Our kid was hyperactive. We were in too much pain to question the book or ask for another opinion.

"Since David was nursing exclusively, I went on the Feingold diet and eliminated foods with dyes and chemicals in them. Just to play safe, I also eliminated milk and egg products in case David was allergic to them. There were days he seemed improved but would then have another reaction. I would play detective and frantically search for the cause of his reactions. I even stopped using toothpaste and wearing lipstick.

"When David was seven months old, I couldn't stand nursing anymore. I was convinced I was poisoning my baby. I hired a nurse for a week to relieve me and to help me wean him. David screamed for ten hours straight while the nurse held him and offered him a bottle. He wouldn't even close his mouth on the nipple. Bill became concerned that the weaning by a stranger was traumatic for David and he wanted it stopped. By that time, I couldn't listen to the baby scream anymore. So I continued to nurse.

"Shortly after we tried to wean, Bill was out of the country for ten days. I was in terrible shape. It was bad enough trying to cope with David with Bill's help, but alone it seemed impossible. Because I was in such bad shape emotionally Dr. K suggested I wean him cold turkey, that is we'd leave David with a nurse for the weekend and he'd be weaned when we returned.

"I must have been a wreck to even consider it. When Bill came home, I pushed him to do it. He was rightfully concerned about the traumatic effect this would have on David. Bill asked the advice of a psychiatrist regarding weaning in this manner and was told to avoid it if possible. During this meeting, the psychiatrist gave Bill more insight into the difficult time I was going through. This helped tremendously. With his added emotional support, I dropped the idea of weaning and was able to pull myself together enough to avoid a breakdown.

"Having a baby can put a strain on a marriage. Having one with colic can push the strongest marriages to the point of divorce. When there's an infant who's miserable for months, the parents' anger has to go some place and it's usually toward each other. Bill hated coming home. I counted the minutes till he got there, then raged at him when he arrived. It was fortunate that we had a strong marriage to begin with and Bill had the maturity to handle a wife who was an emotional wreck.

"During the winter, I was too depressed to take David out very much. To get dressed and take him for a short walk in the buggy took all my strength. Even during those short walks, I'd be terribly tense, waiting for him to start screaming.

"Unfortunately for us, the relatives and friends who could have helped me the most in caring for David live out of town. This was an added burden and made the winter endless.

"David's teething was also a complicating factor in his health. From the time he was six months until he was ten and one half months old he had from four to ten bowel movements a day. Each time he cut a tooth he would begin vomiting a week before and continued until he had the dry heaves on the day the tooth was cut. I can remember changing my clothes several times a day and holding him constantly.

"At ten and one half months, after David finally cut his eighth tooth, we saw a tremendous change in him. He soon began crawling (he never could before) and then at twelve months he began walking. He was so proud of himself and happy. For the first time, I could begin taking him out and enjoy doing it.

"A few days after he cut his teeth, he began eating solids—everything. This turned out to be a mixed blessing. It appeared that his stomach wasn't quite ready for them. At night and during his nap, he developed severe gas pains. He'd awaken every one and one half to two hours screaming. We could hear and smell the gas as he doubled up in pain. Sometimes it would take forty-five minutes to an hour to get him back to sleep. During the day, except for naps, he had much less gas. He probably walked it off. He was in constant motion.

"Obviously, waking up every two hours was incredibly difficult on me but initially, I didn't mind it much. At least I had a happy baby during the day. A happy baby! I began to think I was an okay mother after all.

"David quickly caught up with other babies his age in many areas and I hoped would soon catch up in all others. He was very shy and needed more socialization since he had been in the house so much when he was younger.

"David was still waking up every few hours. The lack of sleep was taking its toll on all of us. I continued blaming his teeth. I thought his molars might be coming in and upsetting his stomach. I convinced myself that once his teeth came in everything would be fine.

"In the meantime, I was still nursing him to sleep and nursing him every time he woke up. Bill and I almost never went out. My daytime schedule depended on when and if David was ready to nap. There were days he never did.

"What I didn't notice were the subtle and gradual changes in David. He was becoming more and more grouchy. He was especially miserable in the morning, and grew more frightened in social situations.

"When he was fifteen months old, David ran a high fever for several days from a viral infection. A week later he ran a high fever again as a reaction to the measles vaccine. We had to hold him and carry him a great deal. When he got well, all he wanted to do was be carried. He had no interest in going outside or playing. He just wanted me to read to him.

"I took David to play group the week after his illnesses. We hadn't been with the group for a month because of his nap schedule. He screamed the entire time.

"I was appalled when I compared him with the other babies. They were younger than David but were far ahead of him developmentally. What was most upsetting was watching those babies sit, concentrate and play with toys. David never played with toys; he was constantly moving.

"I felt like I was kicked in the gut again. There was still something wrong with my baby. Was he hyperactive despite the Feingold diet? Was his behavior due to my mothering?

"Dr. K suggested the Sleep Disorders Center when David was about thirteen months old, but it took me a few months to face the fact that I needed to call. I knew the clinic dealt with parent and child interaction as well as physical disorders and I was too afraid of being criticized. I had convinced myself that David would get better on his own. Bill was afraid the clinic would discover some serious neurological disorder, so he was also reluctant to go.

"We were incredibly fortunate that we finally went. First and foremost, we learned we had a normal baby whose past behavior and lack of social development was due to sleep deprivation, not hyperactivity. Second, we learned we were not alone in our responses to David. Many parents of babies who had colic continue to respond to them as if they were still ill and tend to foster the poor sleep patterns.

"We learned that we had to let David cry it out so he could get the sleep he so desperately needed. This turned out to be much easier than either Bill or I anticipated. But we needed to retrain ourselves before we could retrain David. The doctor gave instructions on every possible contingency, including what to do if David threw up.

"Armed with our instructions, double scotches, frozen pizzas, Haagen Daazs's chocolate ice cream and a few chocolate bars—we were ready for a long night—we put David in bed while he was still awake. Fifteen minutes later, he was asleep! He was only up twice that night for approximately five minutes each time. This was the baby who was up every one and a half hours! David's sleep patterns have backtracked occasionally if he is teething or ill, but his normal pattern now is to sleep through the night, and to take one nap a day.

"Now that David sleeps through the night, we have a rested, happy baby and also a rested, happy mother. Not until I was sleeping through the night did I realize what a toll the sleep deprivation had taken on myself as well as David. We are really a happy family for the first time."

If the change in David's behavior seems unbelievable, remember that this is a mother prone to dramatization. I can attest, however, that trained night crying can sometimes be stopped almost overnight, as it was in this case. Perhaps the child senses in the parents' calm resolve that they really mean business.

The following description from a thirty-three-year-old housewife was given to me six months after a single visit. She describes many of the changes in parental behavior that David's family found useful.

Dan's Mother

"When Dan was born, we knew he was someone very special. From the moment of birth I felt he was quite different from his older brother, Brian. I had hoped one of these differences would be his sleep behavior since Brian slept at least four to six hours *less* per day than any of his peers. Well, his sleep patterns were different from Brian's all right. Unfortunately, they were worse.

"We noticed from the beginning that Dan had always been a very light sleeper, especially for an infant. He would awaken at the slightest sound or disruption. Dan slept through the night (ten hours) for the first time at about one and a half months old. I was thrilled but I knew, based on experience with our first son, that this could be a fluke. It was. That was the only night he did it until he was over eleven months old! From then on, Dan got up every one to three hours each night.

"For the first several months, I nursed him each time he woke thinking he may be hungry since he refused solids. Then we tried other responses; my husband going to him, walking with him, rocking him, even letting him cry. We set up the playpen in our bedroom and put Dan there because he was waking his brother, but Dan invariably awoke when my husband and I came to bed. So we moved his playpen to the family room (farthest from Brian's and our bedrooms). Some nights I would put him in his crib and other nights, when we decided to let him cry, he would go back to the playpen. We were concerned that Dan would wake Brian or vice versa.

"Needless to say, this was wreaking havoc with our lives. I was getting up as many as four to five times per night with Dan. John would get up with Brian if he awoke. On a number of occasions he also got up with Dan. We would both have to be up for the day after 6:00 A.M., when my husband went to work. My fatigue was intensified since I was breastfeeding.

"John and I were always tired. We very often retired as early as 8:00 or 8:30 P.M. to try to catch up on sleep. It didn't help much since we still weren't getting a long stretch of uninterrupted sleep. One advantage John had over me is that he could immediately fall back to sleep during the night. Most times it took me a good half hour or more to get back to sleep. This really was frustrating and gave me even less sleep.

"John and I grew more and more irritable with each other and the children due to fatigue, little or no relaxed time together, and frustration at not being able to solve Dan's problem. Dan was also showing ill effects of his sleep pattern. We knew we had to do something.

"At every baby checkup I mentioned to his doctor that he wasn't sleeping well. At first we discussed it rather casually. I implied that it was not a serious problem. I tend to let things go almost too long before I complain. Then we got to the point where

Dan's doctor felt something should be done. Dan was nearly eight months old, and our doctor was getting concerned not only for Dan but also for me. I had to avoid getting too run down, especially since I had two small children to take care of.

"Dr. H first prescribed Benadryl [dyphenhydramine], an antihistamine, at bedtime. He said this should make Dan drowsy and better able to fall asleep. Nothing changed. We continued this for about a week. Dan has always been, and still is, most difficult when it comes to trying to get medicine, or even food, into him. Unless he can feed himself, he wants no part of it. It was a struggle every night, especially since I wasn't really comfortable giving my child medication when he wasn't sick.

"I called Dr. H again. He felt it was time to use a mild sedative, but he wanted to consult with a pediatrician. The pediatrician concurred with Dr. H's decision, which made me frightened and very upset. Dr. H prescribed Noctec [chloralhydrate, a sedative-hypnotic] at bedtime and during the night if Dan awakened. Both doctors insisted that this drug was not habit-forming. The idea was to get him into a deep enough sleep so that he would not wake as easily during the night.

"I was very uncomfortable with the situation, but that night we tried to get the dosage into Dan. He took about half of it. He *did* fall asleep quicker, but four hours later he woke and continued his pattern of waking every one or two hours through the rest of the night.

"The next day Dan caught a cold. It was my excuse to take him to see Dr. H in person again. He checked Dan out for any possible problems beyond a mild cold but Dan seemed fine.

"The doctor and I talked over my apprehensions about the sedative. I have always avoided medication or drugs if at all possible. Dr. H had seemed to have the same philosophy. I told the doctor that I felt I was being selfish by drugging my son so that *I* could get a night's sleep. He reassured me that we were doing this for *Dan*, that he needed sleep as much as I did. The doctor convinced me—sort of.

"For the next week or so we went back to giving Dan Benadryl in a normal dosage for his cold. As soon as he was healthy again we resumed using the Noctec. It still did no good. Dan would sort of pass out right after he took the medication but then revert to his old pattern after four hours or so. At his nine-month checkup, Dr. H doubled the dosage. We continued this for ten days, and then gave up.

"We were about to schedule an appointment with a pediatric neurologist when a close friend saw a special report on the evening news about children's sleeping problems. From the information I received on the phone and the questionnaire I received, I felt that this, rather than the pediatric neurologist, was the correct next step for Dan.

"Dan was over eleven months old when my husband and I took him to see Dr. Weissbluth. We were very nervous about what he would find, but deep inside I knew there was nothing really wrong with Dan; that he really was normal.

"When the doctor arrived, Dan seemed content, so we went over our questionnaire, answered further questions from the doctor, discussed our thoughts while Dr. W observed Dan.

"The doctor examined him and told us that there was nothing wrong with Dan. Naturally, our response was, 'Great, but why won't he sleep normally? Does he just require very little sleep?' We were told that a child Dan's age needs ten to twelve hours of sleep at night plus one to four hours during the day.

"Dr. W said that Dan seemed to be extremely sensitive to all stimuli and suggested we do the following: take Brian out of the room—his tossing and even his breathing were probably disturbing Dan. Keep Dan's room as dark as possible—take out the nightlight; mount a room darkening shade on the *outside* of the window frame to block out even the light along the edges, and of course, keep the door closed. Take all toys out of his bed and have Dan sleep in a sleeper so that only his hands and head were exposed to rubbing against the sheets. Do no 'noisy' cleaning and turn off phones while Dan slept.

"If Dan still woke up during the night, we were not to go to him. I was concerned that maybe Dan was waking due to hunger. Dr. W said that Dan was the correct height and weight for his age and was not waking because of hunger.

"He warned us that Dan could possibly cry as long as five and one half hours the first night. Before I could verbalize my

thoughts, Dr. W stated them for me. He said that, since I wouldn't
be able to sleep anyway, I should get up and do something such
as take a ride, read a book, watch TV, whatever. Let my husband
handle the situation. This crying would stop within five to seven
days.

"Fortunately, we did not need to experience any of this trauma.
We did all that Dr. W suggested to minimize any stimuli for Dan
during the night. We had only two bedrooms so poor Brian was
put to bed in our room and moved to a sofabed in the family room
when we retired. The situation was obviously far from ideal, but it
worked.

"Dan slept ten and a half hours straight that first night. I was so
exhausted that I slept through also. When I woke at 5:00 A.M., I
wanted to run in and see if Dan was still alive!

"It has been almost six months since then and Dan has slept
through every night. Occasionally he will wake during the night
and cry or call out but we don't go to him and he goes back to
sleep shortly.

"After about two months we decided we should try putting
Brian back in his own room. Poor Brian had gone through a lot
because of Dan's problem; not only was he expected to keep very
quiet when Dan was napping, but he couldn't even sleep in his
own bed!

"The problem was that Dan needed complete darkness with the
door closed, while Brian required a nightlight and the door open.
It took a while but they both got used to having the door open
with the nightlight in the bathroom, out of Dan's view. Dan was in
the relative darkness but Brian could see some light from his bed.
We put Dan to bed with the door closed. Brian goes to bed after
Dan falls asleep and after that the door stays open for the night.

"Dan has his toys back in his bed since he's older and will now
play with them for a while in the morning. He's still a very light
sleeper and we've had to adjust, but things are very good around
here now. We haven't had a group of people over after Dan's
bedtime and we don't keep Dan out past 7:30 or 8:00 P.M.
because we want him to fall asleep in his bed for the night. We
used to be able to put Brian to sleep at someone else's house and
just take him home to his own bed relatively undisturbed. That

would be impossible for Dan. We don't leave the house if it's close to naptime and we get home quickly if we are already out.

"All of these changes have been inconvenient, but well worth the trouble. Things will get even better than they already are. We're having a couple of bedrooms put in upstairs so this will remove Dan further from the first-floor commotion.

"It's amazing what a 'sleep problem' can do to a family. Dan's problem seemed to totally consume our lives. Besides the physical effects to us all through fatigue, it took its toll on our social life as well. We rarely went out in the evening or had people over to our home. We seldom had time to just spend with each other. We were preoccupied, and too darned tired. We were lucky to make it through the day!

"Needless to say, our lives have improved dramatically. We are especially happy that it took no drugs or medication and that nothing is wrong with our son.

"I personally received an added good feeling from all of this. I belong to a parenting support group and the word passed rather quickly that one of my children had a sleep problem that was solved. I have received many calls from mothers who are experiencing trouble with their child's sleep pattern and now I can confidently steer them in the right direction to get help.

Another mother of a very stimulus-sensitive baby was told by her pediatrician to make her baby's bedroom "like a cave." Unfortunately he provided no specific information on how to do this.

The mother, a thirty-year-old artist, wondered if he meant she was supposed to paint stalactites, stalagmites, and bats on the walls! Her comments, below, illustrate how dramatic improvement can occur rapidly, and how important it is for both parents to make careful plans about letting baby alone.

Jackie's Mother

"Everywhere I went people smiled at my baby, Jackie, because she lights up for everyone. People were amazed at how happy she always appeared and how well she behaved. I'd graciously acknowledge their praises but at the same time I'd think to myself: 'Yeah, but if she would only sleep through the night, or even a little during the day!'

"As an infant, Jackie was breastfed, adapted well to any schedule and to my amazement slept through the night. In fact, I remember bragging about it to all my friends who were new mothers and walked around like zombies from exhaustion. Well, my sleep-filled nights were short-lived.

"When Jackie was three months old her sleep habits turned into a nightmare. During the day she took two or three naps which lasted about fifteen minutes apiece. She would stay up until 10:30 P.M., wake up five to eight times for a bottle or diaper change or a half hour of attention. Usually she would to right back to sleep and get up for good at 6:00 or 7:00.

"We were so desperate that we took any advice that was offered. We added cereal to her formula, started early on solids, fed her chamomile tea, eliminated naps in the afternoon, bathed her at night for an hour, gave her massages, took her swimming and then tried the most painful experiment of all: we let her cry for half-hour periods at night before giving her a bottle. We did this for eight straight days with no results. Then for the next two days we let her cry for forty-five minutes at a time. We gave up.

"I hired someone to live in and help me attend to Jackie at night since after two months of interrupted sleep I was unable to function. When Jackie turned eight months, my pediatrician recommended that she take an amino acid with dinner that would act as a sedative. This made me stop and think. I opted for a consultation with Dr. Weissbluth.

"While I was talking with him, Jackie performed one of her fifteen minute naps in her stroller. It was apparent to Dr. Weissbluth that when she awoke she was still very tired. She was living on nervous energy, he said. He pointed out that all babies need about fourteen hours of sleep, so my conclusion that Jackie 'just didn't need that much sleep' was a false notion.

"I mentioned that her father would come home late from work, tip-toe into her room and she would snap out of her sleep immediately to play with him. Jackie always seemed sensitive to noise. A moderately loud sound would make her jump, and if she was sleeping the slightest sound would wake her up.

"Dr. Weissbluth suggested that Jackie's sensitivity to stimuli was the root of her sleeping problems. He said she should sleep in a pitch dark, quiet atmosphere. He said I shouldn't respond to her crying for attention at night as long as she was healthy. He also said I would most likely be up all night the first night and that after three nights it would definitely subside. He said my husband would have to support me in carrying out this plan; that was my main worry.

"When I got home I immediately took Jackie's crib into our den, which has no windows. I put her down for a nap and within two minutes she was sound asleep! She slept for two hours! I was sure the covers were over her head and she was suffocating to death, or that she had jumped out of her crib and was passed out on the floor, but I didn't dare go peek. Jackie woke up smiling, ready to play. I couldn't believe it.

"I explained everything to my husband. He wasn't very convinced that we should just let her cry. I called up a friend of a friend who had had a similar problem with her baby and was claiming that Dr. W's treatment worked. I wanted her to tell my husband of her great results. That finally sold him, so we got set to try it.

"My husband slept at the new house we were building, my housekeeper locked herself in her bedroom and I sat up working in the kitchen, prepared to be up all night.

"We put Jackie down to sleep in the den at 8:00 P.M. She cried for forty minutes and then went to sleep. I worked in the kitchen until 1:30 when it dawned on me that maybe she wasn't going to be up crying all night after all. I heard her whine a few times but she didn't cry until 8:45 the next morning. Three days later she still slept straight through the night from 8:00 P.M. until 7:00 A.M. and took two naps, one from 10:00 to 11:30 A.M., and another from 1:30 to 2:00 P.M. We've all been celebrating ever since."

As these testimonies indicate, older children who do not sleep through the night grind their parents down. It's a long nightmare. These cures may sound miraculous, but I assure you, when the baby and the parents are really ready, their joint bad habit can be broken just this quickly. So please, do not be afraid to leave your children alone at night. You are teaching a health habit: prolonged and uninterrupted sleep . . . for your child and yourselves!

What Should I Do?

Dear parents, when your baby is crying, do nothing. But do nothing deliberately, quietly, gently, confidently and *firmly*. In other words, please try to develop an attitude of:

Purposeful inattention
Studied inattentiveness
Gentle firmness
Constructive resignation
Expectant observation
Watchful waiting

Be attentive to your baby's behavior at night, but try to cultivate a detached and relaxed attitude. As you have read, it does work!

Chapter 14

Love Your Crybaby

Some babies cry a little, some cry a lot. Each day may be different for each baby. During the first few months, nothing about your baby—including crying—will be predictable. At times you may feel thoroughly bewildered.

Relax. After three or four months, things usually calm down. You have read about babies who created havoc in their parents' lives and then developed into sweet little four- and five-month olds. If you accept your crybaby as a dear, wonderful child who will outgrow the crying phase, you will be more relaxed and better prepared to cope with the challenges each day brings.

If your very young baby cries more than three hours most days, if you don't seem to be able to console him, and if this has been going on for several weeks, it may help you to think of him as having a very common, blessedly short-lived condition called colic. I hope you understand more about colic after reading this book.

Do not expect that finding a name for your child's behavior will end your bewilderment. Colic changes from day to day. During the time they suffer from colicky spells, infants may also be erratic in sleeping patterns, irregular in the degree to which they can be consoled, and show great variability in how much they cry. Parents tend to think of colic as a constant state, but I think that in retrospect they focus on the worst nights and let everything blur together. Daily diaries kept by parents show, to the contrary, abrupt and dramatic shifts of behavior and mood. Colic is not as regular or relentless as it may seem.

It will help you and your baby if your can emphasize the good, quiet, calm times. Do not let the 10 percent or 25 percent of your baby's day when she is colicky overshadow the rest.

You may assume, like many people, that your own anxieties are transmitted to your infant and cause him to cry or fuss or sleep poorly. I urge you to put this idea out of your mind. Researchers now know that powerful and complex biologic forces contribute to each baby's behavior, including his crying and sleeping patterns. There are many factors which neither you nor your pediatrician can influence. So the best advice may be as simple as this: be patient and loving during the many difficult hours of the first few months, and don't be afraid to try a few of the techniques which have proven effective for others.

Remember that unexplained crying occurs in all infants during the first few months of life. In only about 20 percent does it become severe enough to be called colic. Despite much conjecture, there has been a striking failure to discover any definite gastrointestinal, allergic, or maternally provoked causes of colic. It may be set off instead by one or more physiological disturbances.

What these physiological causes might be is a question for further study. As I have suggested, they might include disordered regulation of breathing, sleeping patterns which are out of sync with other body rhythms, or abnormal levels of naturally occurring substances such as prostaglandins or progesterone.

There is a great deal that we do not know about a baby's hormones and chemicals, the developing brain, the effects of low birth weight, the control over vital function during sleep and the biological basis for rhythmic patterns. Associations among measurable temperament, sleep patterns, breathing during sleep, and crying suggest that colic may be related to all four. Most likely, colic is the common, final pathway of several related or unrelated disturbances. Solving this mystery will take the work of experts in many fields. Much more cooperative research is needed by the "larks" who observe awake behavior, the "owls" who observe sleeping patterns, and the "hawks" who provoke, prod, and challenge our babies to respond.

Throughout this book I have emphasized that gradations occur in all our measurements: duration of crying spells, sleep durations, temperament ratings, progesterone levels and respiratory pauses during sleep. Is it really necessary to impose labels like Colic and Difficult Temperaments? We researchers desperately want to understand the cause(s) of colic. In order to study, we must divide behavior into categories like normal and abnormal, easy and difficult, or colic and no colic. You as parents should always be thinking of that little *person* — not a condition, a ranking, or a label. When your baby cries at night, remember the smiling, cheerful moments. Focus on everything lovely about her while you help her work out her difficulties. Research can go only so far in understanding the wonders and subtleties of infant behavior. Whatever has been discovered is only meant to be used by parents and pediatricians as seems best for each individual baby, who is like no other.

Hugs, Kisses and Love Help Your Baby Grow

Since my firstborn son's colicky days (and nights!), researchers have learned much about infant behaviors. Would I handle my first son, who had colic, or my second, third, or fourth sons, who did not have colic, any differently now? Absolutely not. The natural course of parenting hasn't changed significantly because of scientific endeavors, although in some cases, recently developed techniques do help. I play with my children and I am tickled when they laugh. I smile when they giggle and I am distressed when they cry. I feel how my children feel and I share their joys and sorrows. I want to love, hug, kiss, caress, tease and wrestle with my children. Love and kisses still are the best treatment for developing an affectionate, giving personality.

Your baby is very speical. Each baby is a miracle. Accept and love your baby with all your heart and all your soul, and be assured that soon your crybaby will become the bundle of joy you hoped for.

Bibliography

Aldrich, C. A., Sing, C., Knop, C. "The Crying in Newly Born Babies. I. The Community Phase." *Journal of Pediatrics* 27 (1945):313-26.

———. "The Crying of Newly Born Babies. II. The Individual Phase." *Journal of Pediatrics* 27 (1945):89-96.

———. "The Crying of Newly Born Babies. III. The Early Period at Home." *Journal of Pediatrics* 27 (1945):428-35.

Aldrich, C. A., Norval, M. A., Knop, C., Vegenas, F. "The Crying of Newly Born Babies. IV. A follow-up Study after Additional Nursing Care Has Been Provided." *Journal of Pediatrics* 28 (1946):665-70.

Anders, T. F. "Night Waking in Infants During the First Year of Life." *Pediatrics* 63 (1979):860-64.

———"Neurophysiologic Studies of Sleep in Infants and Children." *Journal of Child Psychiatry* 23 (1982):75-83.

Becker, P. T., Thoman, E. B. "Intense Rapid Eye Movement During Active Sleep: An Index or Neurobehavioral Instability." *Developmental Psychobiology* 15 (1982):202-10.

Bell, S. M., Ainsworth, M. D. S. "Infant Crying and Maternal Responsiveness." *Child Development* 43 (1972):1171-90.

Bernal, J. F. "Night Waking in Infants During the First 14 Months." *Develop. Med. Child Neurology* 15 (1973):760-69.

Brazelton, T. B. "Crying in Infancy." *Pediatrics* 29 (1962):579-88.

———. *Infants and Mothers*. New York: Delacorte Press, 1969.

Breslow, L. "A Clinical Approach to Colic: A Review of 90 Cases." *Journal of Pediatrics* 50 (1957):196-206.

Boukydis, C. F. Z., Burgess, R. "Adult Physiologic Responses to Infant Cries: Effects of Temperament of Infant, Parental Status, and Gender." *Child Development* 53 (1982):1291-98.

Boulton, T. J. C., Rowley, M. P. "Nutritional Studies During Early Childhood. Incidental Observations of Temperament, Habits, and Experiences of Ill-Health." *Aus. Ped. Journal* 15 (1979):87-90.

Carey, W. B. "Maternal Anxiety and Infantile Colic: Is There a Relationship?" *Clinical Pediatrics* 7 (1965):590-95.

———. "Clinical Application of Infant Temperament Measurements." *Journal of Pediatrics* 81 (1972):823-28.

———. "Night Waking and Temperament in Infancy." *Journal of Pediatrics* 84 (1974):756-58.

———. "Stability and Change in Individual Temperament Diagnosis from Infancy to Early Childhood." *Journal of the American Academy of Child Psychiatry* 7 (1978):331-37.

Carey, W. B., McDevitt, S. C. "Revision of the Infant Temperament Questionnaire." *Pediatrics* 61 (1978):735-39.

Clark, R. L., Ganis, F. M., Bradford, W. L. "A Study of the Possible Relationship of Progesterone to Colic." *Pediatrics* 31 (1963):65-71.

Curzi-Dascalova, L., Gaudebout, C., Dreyfus-Brisac, C. "Respiratory Frequencies of Sleeping Infants During the First Month of Life: Correlations Between Values in Different Sleep States." *Early Human Development* 5 (1981):39-54.

Du, J. N. H. "Colic as the Sole Symptom of Urinary Tract Infection in Infants."*C.M.A. Journal* 115 (1976):334-37.

Emde, R. N., Metcalf, D. "An Electroencephalographic Study of Behavioral Rapid Eye Movement and States in Human Newborns." *Journal of Nervous and Mental Disease* 150 (1970):376-86.

Emde, R. N., Walker, S. "Longitudinal Study of Infant Sleep: Results of 14 Subjects' Studies at Monthly Intervals." *Psychophysiology* 13 (1976):456-61.

Fagioli, I., Salzarulo, P. "Sleep State Development Through 24-Hour Recordings." *Early Human Development* 6 (1982):215-28.

Fish, M., Crockenberg, S. "Correlates and Antecedents of Nine-Month Infant Behavior and Mother-Infant Interaction." *Infant Behavior and Development* 4 (1981):69-81.

Fisichelli, V. R., Karelitz, S., Fisichelli, R. M., Cooper, J. "The Course of Induced Crying Activity in the First Year of Life." *Pediatric Research* 8 (1974):921-28.

Fries, M. "Psychosomatic Relationships Between Mother and Infant." *Psychosomatic Medicine* 6 (1944):159-62.

Grunwaldt, E., Bates, T., Guthrie, D. "The Onset of Sleeping Through the Night in Infancy: Relation to Introduction of Solid Food in the Diet, Birthweight and Position in Family." *Pediatrics* 26 (1960):667-68.

Gunsert, F. "Evaluation of the Efficacy of Dicyclomine Hydrochloride ('Merbentyl') Syrup in the Treatment of Infant Colic." *Curr. Med. Res. Opinion* 5 (1977):258-61.

Harper, R. M., Leake, B., Miyahara, L., Mason, J., Hoppenbrowers, T., Sherman, M. B., Hodgman, J. "Temporal Sequencing in Sleep and Waking States During the First 6 Months of Life." *Experimental Neurology* 72 (1981):294-307.

Hide, D. W., Guyer, B. M. "Prevalence of Infant Colic." *Arch. Dis. Child.* 57 (1982):559-60.

Illingworth, R. S. " 'Three Month' Colic." *Arch. Dis. Child.* 29 (1954):165-74.

———. "Crying in Infants and Children." *British Medical Journal* 1 (1955):75-78.

———. "Evening Colic in Infants: A Double Blind Trial of Dicyclomine Hydrochloride." *Lancet* ii (1959):1119-20.

Jacklin, C. N., Snow, M. E., Gahart, M., Maccoby, E. E. "Sleep Pattern Development from 6 Through 33 Months." *Journal of Pediatric Psychology* 5 (1980):295-303.

Jorup, S. "Colonic Hyperperistasis in Neurolabile Infants." *Acta Paediat.*, Uppsala, Supplement 85 (1952):1-92.

Liebman, W. M. "Infantile Colic: Association with Lactose and Milk Intolerance." *J.A.M.A.* 245 (1981):732-33.

Lounsburg, M. L., Bates, J. E. "The Cries of Infants of Differing Levels of Perceived Temperamental Difficulties: Acoustic Properties and Effects on Listeners." *Child Development* 53 (1982):677-86.

Meyer, J. E., Thaler, M. M. "Colic in Low Birthweight Infants." *American Journal of Dis. Child.* 122 (1971):25-27.

Moore, T., Ucko, L. E. "Night Waking in Early Infancy: Part 1." *Arch. Dis. Child.* 32 (1957):333-42.

Murray, A. D., Dolby, R. M., Nation, R. L., Thomas, D. B. "Effects of Epidural Anesthesia on Newborns and Their Mothers." *Child Development* 52 (1981):71-82.

Onishi, S., Miyazawa, G., Nishimura, Y., et al. "Postnatal Development of Circadian Rhythm in Serum Cortisol Levels in Children." *Pediatrics* 72 (1983):399.

Oseas, R., Phelps, D. L., Kaplan, S. A. "Near Fatal Hyperkalemia from a Dangerous Treatment for Colic." *Pediatrics* 69 (1982):117.

Paradise, J. L. "Maternal and Other Factors in the Etiology of Infantile Colic." *J.A.M.A.* 197 (1966):123-31.

Parmalee, A. H., Schulz, H. R., Disbrow, M. A. "Sleep Patterns of the Newborn." *Journal of Pediatrics* 58 (1961):241-50.

Parmalee, A. H., Wenner, W. H., Schulz, H. R. "Infant Sleep Patterns: From Birth to 16 Weeks of Age." *Journal of Pediatrics* 65 (1964):576-82.

Persson-Blennow, I., McNeil, T. F. "Temperament Characteristics of Children in Relation to Gender, Birth Order and Social Class." *American Journal of Orthopsychiatry* 51 (1971):710-14.

Pierce, P. P. "Delayed Onset of 'Three Months Colic' in Premature Infants." *American Journal of Dis. Child.* 75 (1948):190-92.

Rebelsky, F., Black, R. "Crying in Infancy." *Journal of Genetic Psychology* 121 (1972):49.

Russo, R. M., Gururaj, V. J., Allen, J. E. "The Effectiveness of Diphenhydramine JCI of Pediatric Sleep Disorders." *Journal of Clinical Pharm.*, May-June 1976, pp. 284-88.

Salzarulo, P., Fagioli, I., Salomon, F., Duhamel, J.-F., Ricour, C. "Continuous Feeding and the Waking-Sleeping Rhythm in Children." *Arch. Françaises de Pediatric* 35 (1979):26-32.

Sankaran, K., Conly, J., Boyle, C. A. J., Tyrrell, M. "'Intestinal Colic and Diarrhea as Side Effects in Intravenous Alprostadil Administration." *American Journal of Dis. Child.* 135 (1981):664-65.

Sander, L. W., Stechler, G., Burns, P., Julia, H. "Early Mother-Infant Interaction and 24-Hour Patterns of Activity and Sleep." *Journal of American Academy of Child Psychiatry* 9 (1970):103-23.

Schmitt, B. D. "Infants Who Do Not Sleep Through the Night." *Devel. and Behav. Ped.* 22 (1981):20-23.

Schnall, R., Haan, E. A., Morris, B. D., Smith, A. L. "Infant Colic." *Aus. Ped. Journal,* December 1979.

Shaver, B. A. "Maternal Personality and Early Adaptation as Related to Infantile Colic," in *Psychological Aspects of a First Pregnancy and Early Postnatal Adaptation.* Edited by P. M. Shereshefsky and L. J. Yarrow. New York: Raven Press, 1974, pp. 209-15.

Snow, M. E., Jacklin, C. N., Malcahy, E. E. "Crying Episodes and Sleep Wakefulness Transitions in the First 26 Months of Life." *Infant Behavior and Development* 3 (1980):387-94.

Stewart, A. H., Weiland, I., Leider, A. R., Margham, C. A., Holmes, T. H., Ripley, H. S. "Excessive Infant Crying (Colic) in Relation to Parent Behavior." *American Journal of Psychiatry* 110 (1954):687-94.

Sudell, C. E. "Sleeplessness in Infants." *Practitioner* 109 (1922):89-92.

Taylor, W. C. "A Study of Infantile Colic." *Canadian Medical Association Journal* 76 (1957):458-61.

Thomas, A., Chess, S., Birch, H. G. *Temperament and Behavior Disorders in Children.* New York: New York University Press, 1968.

Thomas, A., Chess, S., Korn, S. J. "The Reality of a Difficult Temperament." *Merrill-Palmer Quarterly* 28 (1982):1.

Thomas, D. B. "Aetiological Associations in Infantile Colic: An Hypothesis." *Aus. Ped. Journal* 17 (1981):292-95.

Weissbluth, M. "Sleep Duration and Infant Temperament." *Journal of Pediatrics* 99 (1981):817-19.

Weissbluth, M., Poncher, J., Given, G., Schwab, J., Mervis, R., Rosenberg, M. "Sleep Duration and Television Viewing." *Journal of Pediatrics* 99 (1981):486-88.

Weissbluth, M. "Modification of Sleep Schedule with Reduction of Night Waking. A Case Report." *Sleep* 5 (1982):262-66.

Weissbluth, M., Brouillette, R. T., Liv, K., Hunt, C. E. "Sleep Apnea, Sleep Duration, and Infant Temperament." *Journal of Pediatrics* 101 (1982):307.

Weissbluth, M. "Chinese-American Infant Temperament and Sleep Duration: An Ethnic Comparison." *Journal of Developmental and Behavioral Pediatrics* 3 (1982):99-102.

Weissbluth, M., Liv, K. "Sleep Patterns, Attention Span, and Infant Temperament." *Journal of Developmental and Behavioral Pediatrics* 4 (1983):34-36.

Weissbluth, M., Davis, A. T., Poncher, J. "Night Waking and Infantile Colic." *Clinical Research* 30 (1982):793A.

Weissbluth, M., Davis, A. T., Poncher, J., Reiff, J. "Signs of Airway Obstruction During Sleep and Behavioral, Developmental and Academic Problems." *Journal of Developmental and Behavioral Pediatrics* 4 (1983):119.

Weissbluth, M., Christoffel, K., Davis, A. T. "Treating Infants with Colic: A Prospective Randomized Trial Using Dicyclomine Hydrochloride." *Clinical Research* 31 (1983):792A.

Weissbluth, M., Green, O. C. "Plasma Progesterone Concentrations in Infants: Relation to Infantile Colic," *Journal of Pediatrics 103* (1983):935-36.

Wender, E. H., Palmer, F. B., Herbst, J. J., Wender, P. H. "Behavioral Characteristics of Children with Chronic Nonspecific Diarrhea." *American Journal of Psychiatry* 133 (1976):20-25.

Wessel, M. A., Cobb, J. C., Jackson, E. B., Harris, G. S., Detwiler, A. C. "Paroxysmal Fussing in Infancy, Sometimes Called 'Colic.' " *Pediatrics* 14 (1954):421-34.

Yogman, M. W., Zeisel, S. H. "Diet and Sleep Patterns in Newborn Infants." *New England Journal of Medicine* 309 (1983):1147.